P9-EDK-415

New Directions for
Teaching and Learning

Marilla D. Svinicki
EDITOR-IN-CHIEF

R. Eugene Rice
CONSULTING EDITOR

Addressing Faculty and Student Classroom Improprieties

John M. Braxton
Alan E. Bayer
EDITORS

Number 99 • Fall 2004
Jossey-Bass
San Francisco

ADDRESSING FACULTY AND STUDENT CLASSROOM IMPROPRIETIES
John M. Braxton, Alan E. Bayer (eds.)
New Directions for Teaching and Learning, no. 99
Marilla D. Svinicki, Editor-in-Chief
R. Eugene Rice, Consulting Editor

Microfilm copies of issues and articles are available in 16mm and 35mm, as well as microfiche in 105mm, through University Microfilms Inc., 300 North Zeeb Road, Ann Arbor, Michigan 48106-1346.

NEW DIRECTIONS FOR TEACHING AND LEARNING (ISSN 0271-0633, electronic ISSN 1536-0768) is part of The Jossey-Bass Higher and Adult Education Series and is published quarterly by Wiley Subscription Services, Inc., A Wiley Company, at Jossey-Bass, 989 Market Street, San Francisco, California 94103-1741. Periodicals postage paid at San Francisco, California, and at additional mailing offices. POSTMASTER: Send address changes to New Directions for Teaching and Learning, Jossey-Bass, 989 Market Street, San Francisco, California 94103-1741.

New Directions for Teaching and Learning is indexed in College Student Personnel Abstracts, Contents Pages in Education, and Current Index to Journals in Education (ERIC).

SUBSCRIPTIONS cost $80 for individuals and $170 for institutions, agencies, and libraries. Prices subject to change. See order form at end of book.

EDITORIAL CORRESPONDENCE should be sent to the editor-in-chief, Marilla D. Svinicki, The Center for Teaching Effectiveness, University of Texas at Austin, Main Building 2200, Austin, TX 78712-1111.

www.josseybass.com

CONTENTS

FROM THE SERIES EDITOR

About This Publication. Since 1980, *New Directions for Teaching and Learning (NDTL)* has brought a unique blend of theory, research, and practice to leaders in postsecondary education. *NDTL* sourcebooks strive not only for solid substance but also for timeliness, compactness, and accessibility.

The series has four goals: to inform readers about current and future directions in teaching and learning in postsecondary education, to illuminate the context that shapes these new directions, to illustrate these new directions through examples from real settings, and to propose ways in which these new directions can be incorporated into still other settings.

This publication reflects the view that teaching deserves respect as a high form of scholarship. We believe that significant scholarship is conducted not only by researchers who report results of empirical investigations but also by practitioners who share disciplined reflections about teaching. Contributors to *NDTL* approach questions of teaching and learning as seriously as they approach substantive questions in their own disciplines, and they deal not only with pedagogical issues but also with the intellectual and social context in which these issues arise. Authors deal on the one hand with theory and research and on the other with practice, and they translate from research and theory to practice and back again.

About This Volume. This issue represents somewhat of a departure from previous practices. In an effort to acknowledge and promote larger-scale research efforts that support the scholarship of teaching, this issue is devoted to the results of just such an effort. The focus is on classroom improprieties, another topic of much interest to all *NDTL* readers, from individual teachers to institutional governing authorities. The research looks at this topic from the perspective of *both* student and faculty behavior and proposes ways to increase the level of civility with which these two groups interact with each other.

Marilla D. Svinicki
Editor-in-Chief

MARILLA D. SVINICKI *is director of the Center for Teaching Effectiveness at the University of Texas at Austin.*

PART ONE

Background

1

This chapter provides a 2X2 model for organizing the effects of both teacher and student improprieties on teaching and learning and puts the subsequent chapters in focus using that model.

Introduction: Faculty and Student Classroom Improprieties

John M. Braxton, Alan E. Bayer

The 1990s were a watershed period for expanded focus and writing on college classroom incivilities. In New Directions for Teaching and Learning no. 77, *Promoting Civility: A Teaching Challenge* (1999), Richardson and contributors focus on approaches that college teachers might employ for addressing student classroom incivility. Unlike much of the earlier writing on classroom problems, which largely addressed cheating and plagiarism, that work broadly focuses on student incivilities, including violence, verbal abuse, and "random acts of passive rudeness" that "plague almost all college teachers" (p. 1). In that volume, Richardson and contributors offer ways for faculty members to manage student incivility and restore student civility.

Also in the 1990s, research and writing began to address faculty as well as student classroom improprieties and the role that faculty incivility may play in prompting student misconduct. Boice (1996) proposes that faculty-initiated classroom incivilities and improprieties in the teaching role are "more common than uncommon" (p. 479), and he claims that traditionally there has been "too large a role [attributed] to students, too small a part to teachers" (p. 484). Subsequently, in our book, *Faculty Misconduct in Collegiate Teaching* (1999), we expressly focus on faculty-initiated improprieties and identify a normative structure that prevails for college undergraduate teachers. We posit that faculty violations of the proscriptive norms that we empirically identified constitute teaching misconduct, or teaching incivilities.

At this point it is important to note that the use of the term *norm* in this issue is derived from its sociological roots. In the sociological sense, a norm can be labeled with phrases that refer to undesirable behavior patterns

NEW DIRECTIONS FOR TEACHING AND LEARNING, no. 99, Fall 2004 © Wiley Periodicals, Inc.

(*proscriptive norms,* such as "the norm of inattentive planning") or phrases that refer to desirable behavior patterns (*prescriptive norms,* such as "the norm of respect for students").

The present NDTL volume extends the previous volume's focus on student incivility to that involving *both* the college student and the college teacher. This builds upon the contributions of Boice (1996) and of *Faculty Misconduct* by concentrating on the following important questions: What sociological theoretical perspectives explain faculty and student improprieties? Are female and minority faculty more likely to experience student classroom incivilities than male and white faculty members? How frequently do faculty members violate undergraduate teaching norms? What types of actions do undergraduate college students take when faculty members exhibit teaching improprieties students regard as most grievous? Do faculty violations of teaching norms harm students as clients of teaching role performance? What impact do students' disruptive behaviors have on faculty teaching performance? What effect do student classroom incivilities have on students? Do students regard classroom incivilities by their classmates as inappropriate behavior?

To the extent that these questions have been addressed at all in previous literature, their grounding in theoretical or conceptual perspectives has generally been poor. Moreover, while some of these questions have a considerable empirical research base, others have been almost totally ignored by any prior research. This volume both reviews and further extends some of the empirical research and begins to offer more theoretical and conceptual frameworks from which to view the dynamics of both faculty and student incivilities as they may affect both the teaching and the learning process.

We begin by providing a schema for guiding future research and discourse on classroom incivilities. As shown in Figure 1.1, the impact of these incivilities is both on the learning process and on teaching performance.

This 2X2 schema provides an organizing concept for this volume. It illustrates the effect of both faculty and student improprieties on teaching performance and on the learning environment. Each cell of the matrix provides an illustrative example of deleterious effects.

The next two chapters of this volume offer theoretical perspectives toward an understanding of student and faculty classroom improprieties. In Chapter Two, Bray and Del Favero describe an array of sociological explanations for faculty and student classroom improprieties. These theories range from functionalism, a classical approach, to such social-psychological perspectives as social control, deterrence, rational choice, social bond, social learning, and labeling theories. The authors also discuss how theories that emphasize the role of the social structure of the larger society—social exchange, anomie, social disorganization, and conflict theory—may also explain faculty and student classroom misconduct.

In Chapter Three, Alexander-Snow argues that female faculty and faculty of color are more likely to experience incivilities from students in their

Figure 1.1. Analytical Schema on the Effects of Faculty and Student Classroom Improprieties

	Effects on Teaching	Effects on Learning
Faculty incivility	Deviant faculty behavior affects one's teaching performance and classroom environment. (For example, intoxication and inadequate course planning yield disorganized instructional content.)	Deviant faculty behavior affects student learning. (For example, faculty cursing, religious bigotry, and personal political commentary detract from an open learning environment.)
Student incivility	Deviant student behavior affects faculty member's classroom performance. (For example, students' disruptive behaviors redirect instructor's activity from education to discipline and authoritarian classroom management.)	Deviant student behavior affects other students' learning opportunities. (For example, a student's insolence and rude interruptions distract other class members from attentiveness to the instructor.)

classrooms than are white male faculty members. Her contention stems from the perspective that cultural identities of students and faculty members alike define an individual's status, role, and place in society. She offers a theoretically informed discussion of how cultural identities work to increase the likelihood that female academics and faculty members of color will experience classroom incivilities by students. She also offers some strategies that these faculty may use to reduce the incidence of student incivilities in their classrooms.

Chapters Four, Five, and Six focus on violations of teaching norms. Chapters Four and Five focus on critical issues pertaining to classroom improprieties committed by college and university faculty members: the extent to which faculty violate teaching norms, the response of students to these violations, and the effects of these violations on students.

In Chapter Four, "Incidence and Student Response to Faculty Teaching Norm Violations," Braxton and Mann assert that, although we can expect some faculty violations of undergraduate college teaching norms, the frequency of such norm violations is unknown. Are they rare or widespread? The authors report the findings of research designed to address this question. Because the social control of faculty teaching improprieties generally requires some action by students (Braxton and Bayer, 1999; Braxton, Bayer, and Noseworthy, 2002), Chapter Four also describes the actions undergraduate college students have taken in response to incidents of teaching norm violations they experienced personally and considered most grievous.

In Chapter Five, Braxton, Bayer, and Noseworthy challenge the assumption that the normative structure of undergraduate college teaching safeguards the welfare of students as clients of teaching role performance (Braxton and Bayer, 1999). They contend that if teaching norms protect the welfare of students, then violations of such norms should adversely affect the academic and intellectual development of students. To address this assertion empirically, the authors report the findings of research that concentrates on the influence of faculty teaching norm violations on student growth and development. They also offer recommendations for policy and practice designed to deter faculty violations of teaching norms.

In Chapter Six, "Toward a Code of Conduct for Undergraduate Teaching," we present ten tenets that an institutional code of conduct should include. These tenets prescribe behaviors college and university faculty members should follow in their teaching. The tenets spring from the norms of undergraduate college teaching we empirically delineated previously (1999). In this chapter, we also offer guidelines for the implementation of a code of conduct for undergraduate college teaching by individual colleges and universities.

Chapters Seven, Eight, and Nine address student norm violations. The first two provide an empirical treatment of issues associated with student classroom incivilities. Chapter Seven concentrates on an empirical delineation of in-class student behaviors that students perceive as highly inappropriate. In this chapter, "Student Norms of Classroom Decorum," Caboni, Hirschy, and Best reason that if we understand which classroom behaviors students perceive as inappropriate, we can begin to understand the type of influence students have on the behavior of their peers within the classroom, specifically as it relates to classroom incivilities. Accordingly, the chapter presents the findings of an exploratory study designed to identify those in-class behaviors perceived as inappropriate by students at one university. The authors also present some implications for policy and practice suggested by their findings.

In his generative article introducing the phenomena of classroom incivilities, Boice (1996) discussed the effects of student classroom incivilities on student classroom behavior and student course ratings. In Chapter Eight, "Effects of Student Classroom Incivilities on Students," Hirschy and Braxton go further, positing that student classroom incivilities may also negatively affect the academic and intellectual development of students and reduce their commitment to their college or university. The chapter recounts the findings of a study that focuses on these questions.

The detection and deterrence of both faculty and student classroom improprieties depend on the existence of public statements that proscribe such behaviors. Chapter Nine outlines a framework for individual colleges and universities to promulgate such public statements. The chapter, "Promulgating Statements of Student Rights and Responsibilities," by Bayer, offers a set of eleven rights that students should expect from the teaching and learning process in general and from faculty members in particular. These rights are offered as illustrative rather than exhaustive of student rights that institutions might promulgate. The author also describes the role of student handbooks in promulgating student rights and responsibilities.

Unlike the focus in much of the New Directions volume *Promoting Civility*, which addresses individual actions of faculty members to address student indiscretion in their particular classrooms, the focus in this volume is on both faculty and students as loci of incivilities and on the possible effects on the enterprise of student learning and in respect to faculty teaching performance.

Finally, in the last chapter, "Conclusions and Recommendations: Avenues for Addressing Teaching and Learning Improprieties," we summarize and expand on the suggestions for policy described or mentioned in the preceding chapters. In all cases, these are options proposed for consideration; they are neither definitive nor exhaustive. Some may be more appropriate in some institutional settings and environments than in others. In addition, to the extent that the chapters in this volume reflect the current status of research and reflection on the interplay of student incivility and instructor misconduct or misjudgment in the collegiate teaching role, they implicitly suggest the next steps needed regarding research on the topic of incivility. Chapter Ten proposes some of the next directions for research on incivility in the collegiate teaching and learning environment, particularly on the synergistic interplay of teacher and student in incidents disruptive to the learning environment, teaching performance, and the learning process.

This volume provides paths that venture into thorny dilemmas. What are college students' rights and responsibilities with respect to fostering an optimal learning environment? How do we reach an appropriate balance between faculty responsibility and autonomy? How do we avoid a repressive or coercive classroom and collegiate environment? How do we best foster the honesty and the civility of students? How do we best promote ethical conduct and integrity among the professoriate? We trust that these difficult questions invite future constructive dialogue among all constituents in the academic community.

References

Boice, R. "Classroom Incivilities." *Research in Higher Education*, 1996, *37*, 453–485.
Braxton, J. M., and Bayer, A. E. *Faculty Misconduct in Collegiate Teaching.* Baltimore: Johns Hopkins University Press, 1999.
Braxton, J. M., Bayer, A. E., and Noseworthy, J. A. "Students as Tenuous Agents of Social Control of Professorial Misconduct." *Peabody Journal of Education*, 2002, *77*, 101–124.
Richardson, S. M. (ed.). *Promoting Civility: A Teaching Challenge.* New Directions for Teaching and Learning, no.77. San Francisco: Jossey-Bass, 1999.

JOHN M. BRAXTON is professor of education in the Higher Education Leadership and Policy Program, Peabody College, Vanderbilt University.

ALAN E. BAYER is professor of sociology, adjunct professor of science studies, and director of the Center for Survey Research at Virginia Polytechnic Institute and State University.

2

To understand the current apparent upsurge in classroom incivility, the authors turn to the literature for possible causes and solutions.

Sociological Explanations for Faculty and Student Classroom Incivilities

Nathaniel J. Bray, Marietta Del Favero

Sociologists devote much of their time and effort to understanding the concept of social organizations within a society, of how groups form and interact, what constitutes acceptable behavior within and among groups, and how the definition of "acceptable" is derived. Impropriety, incivility, and deviance from accepted norms of behavior form one major subset of sociological inquiry. As such, numerous sociological theories have been developed that can help account for faculty and student incivilities in the classroom. So many theories exist, in fact, that uncovering some of their commonalities in explaining incivility is important in pondering their explanatory power vis-à-vis behavior in classrooms of higher education.

This chapter presents several sociological explanations for faculty and student classroom improprieties to illustrate how these theories can be (and in some cases, have been) brought to bear on the topic of incivility in classrooms of higher education. The theoretical explanations we consider range from those incorporating classical approaches (such as functionalism) to those based on social-psychological approaches (social control, deterrence, and rational choice models; social bond, social learning, and labeling theories) and those with a greater perspective on social culture and structure (social exchange, anomie, social disorganization, and conflict theory; see Akers, 1997). In this chapter we highlight some of the key elements of the more popular theories and note key points of overlap. We then link these theories to the faculty and student norms described in the works of Boice (1996) and Braxton and Bayer (1999) and offer propositions for future study.

Nature of Incivilities in Classrooms of Higher Education

There are several possible causes for classroom incivilities. Using student cheating as an example, Michaels and Miethe (1989) cited parental pressure for better grades, encouragement from friends, failure to study properly, and opportunity to cheat without detection as possible reasons for cheating. Yet cheating constitutes only one form of classroom incivility among only one of the classroom stakeholder groups. From work by Boice (1996) and Michaels and Miethe (1989) we know student incivilities also to include talking loudly when others are speaking, tardiness, early departure from class, and sarcasm aimed at the teacher. Faculty incivilities found by Braxton and Bayer (1999) in their empirical work include condescending negativism, inattentive planning, moral turpitude, particularistic grading, personal disregard, uncommunicated course detail, and uncooperative cynicism.

There is an interactional effect between students and faculty in the classroom; incivilities are not unidirectional, nor do they occur in a vacuum. Faculty and student misconduct are interlocking phenomena (Braxton and Bayer, 1999). As such, a history of poor interaction and suboptimal relations may build within the classroom that can ultimately yield incivilities where no evidence of any impropriety may have originally existed. We can stipulate that violations of normative classroom behavior can inhibit learning (Braxton and Bayer, 1999). Therefore, it is important to study these norms in order to bring greater understanding to their deterrence.

While deviancy can inhibit learning, a functionalist perspective purports that deviance is necessary within a group, an essential probing and pushing of social boundaries that forces members of a society or those in social organizations to question its values. Without some social agitation, institutions of higher education would not have made the great steps in social justice and equity that they have made (see, for example, Boren, 2001). But while deviance may at times be helpful in ensuring intellectual stimulation and growth, at other times this incivility can serve to enhance some areas valued by a society to the detriment of others (Durkheim, 1982). For instance, in the norms outlined by Braxton and Bayer in Chapter Six of this volume, inattentive planning and uncooperative cynicism on the part of faculty may be in part due to a desire to focus more heavily on their research role that may in turn provide social benefit. Functionalism, however, is a sociological approach on the wane in higher education. Other sociological theories have arisen that can prove very fruitful in explaining classroom incivilities.

Social Control, Deterrence, and Rational Choice Models

Some sociological theories focus on why people choose not to deviate from accepted norms of behavior, especially in instances where it may serve their own ends. Faculty who refuse to shave a little time off of their course preparation or who grade without particular attention to detail despite heavy demands on their time, or students who won't slide into class late or leave early because of other commitments may fit this model.

Social Control Theories. Social control theories focus on the social mechanisms in place to explain the pressures that keep people from engaging in these behaviors despite their appeal (Hirschi, 1969). Control theorists focus their attention on the factors that prevent deviance. The general concept here is that people may often be expected to follow the route leading to maximum personal gain. As such, the area of interest in control theory is what keeps people from violating social norms when it may be in their own interest to do so (Hirschi, 1969). A control theorist therefore views deviance as a lack of adequate socialization into the culture. Faculty may focus on research to the reduction of teaching preparation, an approach consistent with the emphasis on research in their graduate training that is not readily mediated by the organizational socialization of new faculty. This notion of why individuals do not deviate even when it may be in their own interest to do so is integral to our choice of deterrence and rational choice theories in explaining faculty and student classroom conduct.

Deterrence Theory. Deterrence theory (see Akers, 1997; Gibbs, 1975) posits that behaviors are stopped by the perceived probability and severity of punishment for engaging in the behavior. Consider the example of student cheating. Students would conceivably gain certain rewards (better grades, and so on) for engaging in this deviant behavior. According to deterrence theory, incivilities in the classroom are mediated by the perception of being caught or of the punishment likely to be encountered for a behavior. Certainly, cheating may be one such incivility in the classroom, but the punishment for being caught can be very high. However, what about a slightly less extreme instance? Students or faculty members arriving late to class may be frowned upon but the social stigma may be lower. And the threshold may be lowered over time. The infamous "fifteen-minute walk rule," in which students feel they have the right to leave the class if the faculty member is more than fifteen minutes late, has been mentioned in more than one classroom. And students in current educational settings can often be seen wandering in and out of classrooms or talking about non-course-related topics during class discussions.

In such settings, deterrence theories would argue that incivilities arise because the perception or likelihood of punishment is low, or that the severity of the punishment is also low. In essence, the higher the cost incurred by engaging in a certain behavior, the less likely the behavior is to occur. This view is supported by Michaels and Miethe's findings (1989) that self-reported instances of cheating among students decreased as their perception of the probability of being caught increased. Faculty and students thereby create the classroom culture in which incivilities occur. This suggests that if faculty police rigorously for cheating efforts, students would be deterred from engaging in cheating behaviors. Other behaviors, such as talking in class when the professor is lecturing, or tardiness, may also be deterred should they be noticed and subsequent efforts made to root out the behavior. Indeed, the deterrence need not come from the faculty member—students themselves, should they find the behavior inappropriate, may take action to deter those behaviors that interfere with their own values or learning.

Rational Choice Theory. This theory (see Akers, 1997; Pialivin, Gartner, Thornton, and Matsueda, 1986) is closely related to deterrence theory, with one major adjustment. Like deterrence theory, rational choice models consider why people do not engage in impropriety or incivility. Unlike deterrence theory, however, rational choice theory takes into account not only the punishment for being caught in inappropriate behavior but also the possible rewards for the behavior. Rational choice models picture a logical decision-making process of when and whether to engage in inappropriate actions. For students desiring that extra ten minutes' sleep, the reward of feeling a bit more rested may simply outweigh the costs associated with late arrival to class. Again, in considering student cheating, Michaels and Miethe (1989) found that cheating increased as perceived benefits outstripped perceived costs (specifically, likelihood of detection and severity of response if detected). Further support can be found in Sletta (1992), who posited that social interactions involve a calculation of rewards and costs by participants. Mutual rejection or hostility, such as that associated with classroom incivility, may dominate the relationship where perceptions of low rewards or high costs exist.

Consider an example from a setting not related to higher education. When faced with high murder rates and other hostile crimes, New York City police made a conscious effort not just to target assaults and felonies, but to increase focus on all crimes, instituting a zero-tolerance policy. In doing so, New York acted according to what has been termed a "broken windows" mentality (Wilson and Kelling, 1982), in which even relatively minor street crime (or incivility) could scare the populace off the streets and ultimately attract even more violent criminal activity. In the thinking behind deterrence and rational choice theories, a zero-tolerance action then would give possible perpetrators pause, as the likelihood of punishment and the severity of that punishment would be elevated. The reward would simply be outstripped by potential cost. In New York City, the effect was a reduction in violent crime, but with a dramatic rise in claims of police brutality and incivility (Green, 1997).

Does the "success" (as it was termed by the New York officials) of such a zero-tolerance policy mean that faculty members and students need to move to a strict style of zero-tolerance enforcement of incivilities in the classroom? Deterrence theory and rational choice theory would both argue that the more faculty and students pay attention to and place sanctions against incivilities in the classroom, the less likely they are to occur. However, as in the example above, there may be a reduction in classroom civility as a backlash as well. The theories described next offer some explanations of why that occurs and allow for other possible considerations.

Anomie and Social Disorganization Theory

The use of deterrence and rational choice theories to consider classroom incivilities leaves out an important aspect of the classroom dynamic—the special bond between students and other students, and between students and the faculty member. Anomie (sometimes referred to as strain theory) and social bond theory look not just at punishment and reward but also at the feelings of commonality, attachment, commitment, involvement, and belief within a social group or setting.

Anomie. As posed by Durkheim (1951), anomie posits a certain "normlessness" in society. Anomie often arises in a society growing increasingly complex, as there are fewer and fewer commonalities binding people together. As a result, people feel less attached to the society and less bound by its rules. Merton (1938) furthered these ideas, arguing that anomie really refers to the disconnect between the ends valued by a society and the means accepted to achieve those ends. If all people in a society are trained to seek personal goals, such as good grades or success, that not all may attain, normlessness and a sense of strain may result (Merton, 1938, 1968). In his means-ends schema, Merton proposes five responses to strain that may be considered in viewing classroom incivility: conformity, innovation, rebellion, retreatism, and ritualism (that is, strict adherence to norms). Under this way of viewing classroom behavior, the student behaviors of insolent inattention and disrespectful disruption, as are outlined by Braxton, Bayer, and Noseworthy in Chapter Five, may be considered to result directly from students feeling removed from the educational franchise. This may be especially true for those who do not share the same legitimate access to the ends sought. Merton's postulations indicated that those with lower socioeconomic status would have increased tendencies toward deviance. In higher education, student goals are high grades and pursuit of excellence; in other words, to stand apart from the crowd. Some fields with curved scoring methods ensure that some will excel and many will not. In such an environment, a certain normlessness may be expected among students who feel disconnected. Grade inflation and reduction of curved grading scales may also be a result of such an environment. On the faculty side, pressure to publish and the perceived weight of publishing in tenure decisions may cause faculty to retreat from their teaching responsibilities and focus more of their effort on research.

Social Disorganization. In a vein similar to anomie theory, the position of social disorganization theorists is that rapid changes in a society or group (such as those that result from immigration or industrialization) can cause a change in social values such that the behavior patterns of the people in the group are changed (Akers, 1997; Shaw and McCay, 1942; Traub and Little, 1994). College is often a period of exploration and self-discovery for students as they seek to fit in with peer groups on campus. Failure to cope with the transition may cause students to reduce attention to their educational pursuits and may lead to classroom incivility. Student apathy and disinterestedness can yield tardiness, sarcasm toward professors who cannot seem to relate, cheating to "just get the grade," or outright withdrawal. Social disorganization theory then explains classroom incivility as a condition associated with the effects of college on the psychosocial development of students.

Social Exchange Theory

As in rational choice approaches, social exchange theory incorporates the behavior-reward association. Like anomie and social disorganization, notions of social exchange incorporate a sense of commonality, or mutuality, among participants to social action. Traditional social exchange theory focuses on the social relation as the unit of analysis. This theory suggests that learning, both in and outside the classroom, is a process of exchange among class participants. Learning can be seen as focusing on dyadic or multi-party exchanges (Blau, 1994; Homans, 1974) where the relationship is defined by reciprocity, value, mutuality, and influence. Where mutuality is not upheld, the relationship is diminished. We posit that it is such a diminution in the relationship between faculty and students that leads to uncivil behavior.

The exchange concept is consistent with Boice's view (1996) that faculty and students are partners in the generation of uncivil behavior. As with the value component of rational choice theory, their behaviors in the classroom can be thought of as interdependent exchanges of value. A faculty member awards good grades in exchange for good performance by a student and has an expectation of a positive evaluation in exchange for good teaching. A student expects that if she performs well a good grade will be forthcoming. Social exchange theory posits that when these expectations are not met there is a high likelihood that the relationship will not continue. Homans (1974) asserts, in fact, that unless both parties are profiting, the exchange will not continue. In a classroom setting, however, where termination of the exchange may not be an option, hostility or uncivil behavior on the part of students or faculty can result. On the faculty side, negligent advising, particularistic grading, or uncooperative cynicism may result. Students perceiving their exchange with the instructor to be unprofitable may resort to uncivil behavior. Such behavior undermines learning.

Key concepts in the exchange process—reinforcement, resources, rewards, and costs, according to Emerson (1976), can be used as analytic tools to understand exchange relations in the classroom context. The manner in which faculty communicate course material or provide feedback to students' class participation can reinforce or diminish students' learning or academic self-concept. Similarly, student displays of learning and academic progress can serve as reinforcement for faculty in their teaching role. The instructor is an information resource for students, while students' perspectives serve as resources for faculty in gauging student learning and in informing their research. Students seek a high grade as a reward for their participation in the course, while faculty stand to be rewarded where positive teaching outcomes are recognized. Costs to faculty occur when a student exits class early (negative stimulus) or misses an appointment, resulting in interrupted or forgone effort on other activities, such as research. One of the most common costs to faculty of improprieties in their interactions with students is no doubt the risk of poor teaching evaluations should students view their classroom behavior negatively. The ultimate cost to students of their own incivility is an unsatisfactory course grade.

Social Bond Theory

Social bond theory is often considered a social control theory. However, the theory has broadened beyond the tenets of deterrence and rational choice theory to include a few important differences. Like anomie theory, social bond theory focuses on the weakening of social ties within a society or group. While anomie focuses on the disconnect or departure from society, social bond theory focuses on four major areas of unity or bonding among individuals that prevent or moderate inappropriate behavior: attachment, commitment, involvement, and belief (Hirschi, 1969). To link this theory to the impropriety of cheating as studied by Michaels and Miethe (1989), attachment to a peer group that is law-abiding reduces the likelihood of wrongdoing. Commitment refers to the stake one has in remaining faithful to dictates of appropriate behavior. Involvement is a measure of level of engagement in conventional activities. Belief refers to the level of certainty one has that appropriate behavior is in fact appropriate. These four bonds can help constrain classroom incivility.

The efforts described in rational choice and deterrence theories of closely guarding and policing behavior within the classroom may in fact temper behavior. But the use of such tactics also runs the risk of reducing the strength of the social bond by reducing the level of trust and shared concern within the classroom. Instead, such external monitoring creates an "us against them" mentality that can typify anomie. Indeed, anomie and social bond theory seem to have strong roles in classroom cheating. Michaels and Miethe (1989) recounted students' reports that a strong attachment to peers who cheat significantly increased the likelihood of one's own cheating. The belief that the behavior was not very serious also had a significant impact on their behavior.

The peer attachment effects with regard to cheating can be applied to other forms of incivility as well, including excessively boisterous or inopportunely timed side conversations, persistent late arrival or early departure, and attending class unprepared. Strong attachment to peers engaged in these behaviors would increase one's own likelihood of behaving in such a manner.

Social Learning Theory

One of the important elements highlighted in the social bond and anomie theories is that the faculty and students do not necessarily link to some monolithic, overall institutional or societal culture. The byplay among those groups forms the focus of social learning theory; the center of interest within this theory is how individuals behave differently based on their level of commitment and attachment to various groups to which they belong (Akers, 1985). People belong to several groups at once, many of which have competing cultures and values. Their differing levels of attachment and engagement within those groups, including the classroom as one culture, play a role in the level of their classroom incivility as well as their perceptions of that behavior. In other words, two of the most important factors in determining the level of classroom incivility according to this theory are the beliefs and behaviors of one's closest peers. The student's differential association with his or her primary peer group reinforces deviancy from societal, or in this case classroom, norms of behavior. This in turn can lead the student to develop a definition of what is acceptable behavior that does not agree with the society beyond the primary group. Michaels and Miethe (1989) found this model to have strong predictive power, in that students associated with subgroups more heavily engaged in cheating were themselves more likely to cheat than the larger group of their classroom peers.

Conflict and Labeling Theories

With attributes akin to ideas of social disorganization, conflict theory (Akers, 1997) offers the view that a society or an organization exists in a constant state of flux, with various interests and values competing in setting the direction of the group. The negotiation of social function and values among participants is vital in this picture. The more powerful group stands to make the rules, leaving the less-influential group or groups to be in conflict with so-called accepted values. For example, faculty are charged by position with the function of guiding student learning, which includes determining what will be covered in the course, how students will demonstrate their learning, and how those demonstrations of learning will be evaluated. In this sense faculty hold the power. Students may be co-participants in this function to a greater or lesser degree depending on the amount of power faculty assign to them. The extent to which the power differential plays into the function students perform in course learning determines whether conflict occurs. Inattention and disruption on the part of some students, a focus on discussing personal events or interests rather than focusing on the class, for instance, may conflict with the desire of other students to learn the material and of the faculty to help foster learning. Students thus have some power over the faculty member as well. Hence, in the case of classroom incivility, faculty and student power differentials interact to guide the flow of the class.

Labeling theory has much in common with conflict theory (see also Akers, 1997; Traub and Little, 1994). Labeling theory again focuses on the manner in which the incivility or impropriety comes to be viewed as inappropriate. According to this theory, behaviors are not inherently inappropriate. Instead, those in a society or members of a social organization label certain behaviors as undesirable. Of course, it is those in positions of power within the culture who play the strongest roles in defining which behaviors will be considered uncivil. In the classroom then, the power differential would seem to indicate that faculty would be in the position to label what behaviors were uncivil. Students as peers have some social interaction and collective power that allow them to help label behavior as appropriate or inappropriate. Students may in fact collectively label not only their peers' behavior as inappropriate, but faculty behavior as well when it violates their expectation. However, it may be important to mediate this view with the realization that student and faculty peers may have the most listened to voice in labeling classroom incivility.

Conclusion

Sociological theories have a lot to offer in accounting for student and faculty classroom incivilities. While many theories exist, several main concepts resonate across them. Students and faculty are members of many social groups in addition to that of the classroom. Their peer groups and primary social groups affect them beyond the influence of the larger society. While they do come from different backgrounds, it is vital that faculty and students learn to negotiate together the rules for appropriate behavior in the classroom. Faculty and students should share common expectations of what constitutes appropriate classroom behavior for both groups. Consistency is a key to this common understanding.

Control theories focus on why people do not deviate when it may be in their best interest to do so. Anomie and social bond theories focus on the links of individuals with their society or their organization. Social learning theory considers the differential association of the individual with primary social groups versus society or the classroom as a whole.

These variegated, yet overlapping, theories not only help explain how classroom incivilities arise, but also offer some ideas on how they can be handled. Each of the theories described here has some power for understanding how faculty behavior can or does affect student incivility, as well as how student behaviors can affect faculty or other students as well. However, it is not possible to say one theory is more powerful or appropriate in describing student or faculty incivilities. Instead, each theory focuses on some elements of the social organization and dynamic, each of which may be important within a given environment. More empirically based research using these theories in the classroom may help determine if some are more predictive or stronger than others across social organizations. With this in mind, we make some propositions to consider in using these theories.

Propositions

Our review of sociological theories applicable to faculty and student classroom improprieties suggests to us the following propositions for future empirical examination.

Deterrence theory suggests that faculty policies designed to discourage late class arrivals, missing classes, and early exit by students will result in lower occurrences of these behaviors. Regarding faculty behavior, deterrence theory suggests that improper classroom behavior will be deterred if faculty perceive there is a cost or punishment associated with it, such as through student warnings or evaluations.

From a rational choice perspective, student late arrival to class, cutting classes, and early exit, and faculty engagement in Braxton and Bayer's inviolable and admonitory norms (1999; described in Chapters Four through Six) will be lessened where the perceived costs for such behavior outweigh the rewards. The relationship holds true for faculty as well.

Conflict theory suggests that constructive faculty or student attempts to diminish the faculty-student power differential in the classroom will result in diminished student incivility.

Anomie and social disorganization theories suggest that co-curricular activities designed to enhance students' coping skills will result in diminished uncivil classroom behaviors.

Consistent with social exchange theory, where student-faculty interactions are mutually rewarding, classroom improprieties will be less likely to occur.

From a social learning and social bonding perspective, students and faculty members bond with various peer groups that represent subsections of the larger campus culture and society in general. As such, student and faculty incivility are linked to the extent to which they believe the behavior would be accepted by their peers.

The conceptual approaches presented in this chapter are intended to inform frameworks for future research into this understudied area for which Boice's classroom incivilities (1996) and Braxton and Bayer's inviolable and admonitory norms (1999) have laid a solid foundation. Further, by situating faculty and student behavior within relevant sociological contexts, we hope that the theoretical formulations presented in this chapter will lead educators to insights into ways classroom incivilities can be minimized, if not ultimately prevented.

References

Akers, R. L. *Deviant Behavior: A Social Learning Approach.* (3rd ed.) Belmont, Calif.: Wadsworth, 1985.

Akers, R. L. *Criminological Theories: Introduction and Evaluation.* (2nd ed.) Los Angeles: Roxbury, 1997.

Blau, P. *Structural Contexts of Opportunities.* Chicago: University of Chicago Press, 1994.

Boice, R. "Classroom Incivilities." *Research in Higher Education, 37,* 1996, 453–485.

Boren, M. E. *Student Resistance: A History of the Unruly Subject.* Independence, Ky.: Routledge, Taylor and Francis, 2001.

Braxton, J. M., and Bayer, A. E. *Faculty Misconduct in Collegiate Teaching.* Baltimore: Johns Hopkins University Press, 1999.

Durkheim, E. *Suicide.* (J. A. Spaulding and G. Simpson, trans.). New York: Free Press, 1951.

Durkheim, E. *The Rules of Sociological Method.* (S. Lukes, trans.). New York: Free Press, 1982.

Emerson, E. "Social Exchange Theory." *Annual Review of Sociology,* 1976, 2, 335–362.

Gibbs, J. *Crime, Punishment, and Deterrence.* New York: Elsevier, 1975.

Green, M. "Testimony of the Public Advocate Before the New York City Council Committee on Public Safety." September 11, 1997.

Hirschi, T. *Causes of Delinquency.* Berkeley: University of California Press, 1969.

Homans, G. C. *Social Behavior: Its Elementary Forms.* (revised ed.) Orlando: Harcourt, Brace, 1974.

Merton, R. K. "Social Structure and Anomie." *American Sociological Review,* 1938, 3, 672–682.

Merton, R. K. *Social Theory and Social Structure.* New York: Free Press, 1968.

Michaels, J. W., and Miethe, T. D. "Applying Theories of Deviance to Academic Cheating." *Social Science Quarterly,* 1989, 70(4), 870–885.

Pialivin, I., Gartner, R., Thornton, G., and Matsueda, R. L. "Crime, Deterrence, and Rational Choice." *American Sociological Review,* 1986, 51, 101–119.

Shaw, C., and McCay, H. D. *Juvenile Delinquency and Urban Areas.* Chicago: University of Chicago, 1942.

Sletta, O. "Social Skills as Exchange Resources." *Scandinavian Journal of Educational Research,* 1992, 36(3), 183–190.

Traub, S. H., and Little, C. B. *Theories of Deviance.* (4th ed.) Itasca, Ill.: Peacock, 1994.

Wilson, J. Q., and Kelling, G. L. "Broken Windows: The Police and Neighborhood Safety." *The Atlantic Monthly,* 1982, 249(3), 29–38.

NATHANIEL J. BRAY *is research analyst in the Department of Institutional Planning and Research Analysis at Virginia Tech.*

MARIETTA DEL FAVERO *is assistant professor of education in Louisiana State University's College of Education Department of Educational Leadership, Research, and Counseling.*

Classroom incivility is influenced by many factors. This chapter identifies three that are commonly thought of as influencing the degree to which students will engage in inappropriate behaviors in the classroom.

Dynamics of Gender, Ethnicity, and Race in Understanding Classroom Incivility

Mia Alexander-Snow

Little research has been conducted on the causes of and solutions for student classroom incivility. We know that classroom incivility is experienced to some degree by all teachers. However, to what extent do ascribed characteristics—of students and faculty—such as race, sex, and ethnicity, influence the occurrences of student classroom incivility? Is there a greater likelihood for female faculty and faculty of color to experience classroom incivility than their white male counterparts?

Boice's Study of Classroom Incivility

After conducting a five-year study of classroom incivility at a large, public university in an urban setting, Boice (1996) asserted that classroom incivility was more common than uncommon, occurring in more than two-thirds of the courses he tracked, and was particularly acute for those teachers whom students perceived as aloof and indifferent to student needs. Continued persistence of classroom incivility resulted in the divestment of both teacher and students; teachers became less enthused about their students and their course, and students became less involved in the classroom experience (as demonstrated by students coming late and leaving early, making sarcastic remarks or gestures, and so on). Consequently, courses reflecting high classroom incivility correlated with poor course evaluations and poor student performance. Students attributed their non-involvement and mediocre classroom experience to teacher incompetence, and teachers attributed poor student performance and negative course evaluations to student apathy. Boice concluded that "the key initiator of classroom incivility may be teachers' deficits in immediacies (i.e., expressions of warmth and approachability) particularly in the first few days of classes," (p. 453) and that increased teacher immediacy behaviors resulted in lower levels of classroom incivility.

Overall, Boice's findings are helpful, shedding greater light on the possible causes and solutions for classroom incivility; however, the call for teachers to display more immediate behaviors is too simplistic as a response to such a complex phenomenon.

Purpose of This Chapter

The purpose of this chapter is to build on Boice's research by adding the contextual dimension, particularly as it relates to female faculty and faculty of color. I argue that researchers cannot observe classroom incivility without taking into account the role of cultural perceptions and social power when prescribing the degree of immediacy needed for a teacher to create a classroom experience conducive to positive student involvement. I address the following questions: How much of a role do cultural perceptions, defined by expected social norms, expectations, and stereotypes, affect the level of immediacy between students and their teachers? How do these perceptions affect the classroom dynamic? Who wields the power base? How does the basis of power affect the degree of immediacy shown by teachers and level of classroom incivility?

Since this chapter is theoretically based, my analysis draws from the theoretical constructs and studies prominent in the field of cross-cultural communication and in social theories. Having established the theory, I expand on Boice's research findings (1996) by adding the missing pieces that provide greater context for examining the role of cultural perceptions in shaping the classroom dynamic between students and their teachers, particularly female faculty and faculty of color.

Finally, I incorporate strategies for reducing the level of classroom incivility to the point where classroom incivility can be a constructive force, aiding teachers, particularly female faculty and faculty of color. I do not discuss every possible scenario with each typifying example Boice presents; however, I do examine those examples that best illustrate the indirect influence that cultural perceptions, defined by stereotypes and social power, may have in fostering classroom incivility, illustrating that the term *immediacy* and the concept of power have cultural implications that are affected by persons' ascribed characteristics, such as sex, race, and ethnicity.

Assumptions and Terms

There is a notable lack of research on current gender stereotypes, on beliefs about the speech of people of color, and on the influence of gender and race on speech stereotypes. Traditionally, normative behavior for males and females has varied among white Americans, African Americans, Native Americans, and Hispanic Americans (Banks, 2003). Therefore, stereotypes are used in this chapter for discussion purposes about group and cultural behaviors. In this chapter the term *white* denotes Americans of European descent, *African American* refers to persons of African descent born in the United States, and *people of color* refers to those groups in America (African Americans, Asian Americans, Latino Americans, and Native Americans) that have historically been oppressed by the dominant white culture. The term *culture,* unless otherwise noted, should be understood to embody whiteness; as it holds the power and authority in society, white culture is the dominant or normative culture to which all other cultures are subordinate.

Race is a socially determined category that is related to physical characteristics (skin color, eye shape, and so forth) (Banks, 2003). Ethnicity reflects a person's group identity based on national origin, language, religion, or food; it is not based on biological traits (Banks, 2003; Schofield, 2003). Racism and sexism exist. Each has a form of oppression associated with it. Racism is a system of advantage based on race; sexism is a system of advantage based on sex. Both systems are based on the systematic oppression of persons of color and females, in which cultural messages and institutional policies and practices operate to the advantage of white males (Tatum, 1997).

Given that most cultural communication theory and research have focused on the gender, race, and speech style stereotypes between and among African Americans and white Americans, the discussion and examples in this chapter largely reflect the racial and ethnic experiences of African American and white American males and females. However, when reference is made to persons of color or brown-skinned persons, generalizations can be made to include people of color.

Understanding Culture and Cultural Perceptions

Erickson (2003) defines culture as "A sedimentation of the historical experience of persons and of social groupings of various kinds, such as nuclear family and kin, gender, ethnicity, race, and social class, all with differing access to power in society" (p. 32). Communication theorists Wood and Dindia (1998) extend Erickson's definition of culture by emphasizing the role communication has in the invention and sharing of culture: "Women and men, like people everywhere, learn rules, meanings, and norms of communication and social life through interaction with others in particular contexts and. . . . different social groups, or communication cultures, inculcate distinct styles of being, knowing, and communicating. By extension, individuals may learn new rules, meanings, and forms of communication if they participate in communication cultures that foster skills and perspectives different than those they learned previously" (p. 60).

Three assumptions are implicit in these definitions. First, everyone in the world is cultural, even though not all culture is equal in power and prestige (for example, white culture is the hegemonic culture in the United States). Second, all people have multiple cultural identities (such as Jewish American female or middle-class African American male). Third, human interaction is cultural, continually shaped and reshaped by social context (Alfie, 1988; Erickson, 2003; Tusmith and Reddy, 2003; Wood and Dindia, 1998). Who we are, what we desire, and how we view ourselves and others are shaped by the explicit and implicit cultural messages we learn through sustained social discourse.

Cultural perceptions are based on the interpretation of meaning and behavior within a given social context. Since individuals reflect multiple cultural realities, so do they also reflect multiple social realities such that there is no single interpretation of human behavior. In other words, as Hart and Morry (1997) state, "The same behavior performed by persons of different social characteristics or from different cultural backgrounds is likely to be interpreted as having different meaning" (p. 34). What is of most importance in understanding culture and cultural perceptions is that the inherent social and cultural inequities between and among subcultures define individual perceptions and cultural realities. The socio-cultural identities are hierarchical, defining individuals' social place, role, and status. For example, although a white female is a member of the subordinated group, women, her white cultural status may elevate her to a higher social standing than an African American woman from a lower social class.

Cultural perceptions are defined by stereotypes and social power. To the extent that some hold stereotyped beliefs about men, women, and people of color, these beliefs can lead them to differential expectations about how people should behave based on their cultural identities (Aries, 1996). Differences attributed to individuals' cultural identities may, in fact, reflect socially structured inequities in the power accorded to and experienced by subordinated groups (Wood and Dindia, 1998). These cultural identities reflect the social, economic, and political characteristics of society and have an impact on how individuals are perceived and how others respond to them (Schofield, 2003). Research on ethnic stereotyping has shown that in American society more negative characteristics (such as "slow," "lazy") are ascribed to persons with black and brown skin than persons with light or white skin (who are more likely to be ascribed positive characteristics such as "ambitious," smart") (Hart and Morry, 1997). In a study of communication stereotypes, Popp, Donovan, Marsh, and Peele (2003) reported that white college students perceived African American speech to be loud, ostentatious, aggressive, active, argumentative, hostile, open, critical, and straightforward. Furthermore, research has shown that African American and Puerto Rican women do not accept the traditional white female stereotypes, attributing more masculine characteristics to themselves than do white women (Crawford, 2001).

Men and women speak in different ways as a result of differences in social power (Tannen, 1990). Men are believed to have demanding voices, to be dominating, authoritarian, to the point, blunt, forceful, aggressive, and boastful. Women are believed to speak politely, gently, rapidly, and emotionally, and to show more concern for the listener (Edelsky, 1976; Kramarae, 1981; Lakoff, 1973; Siegler and Siegler, 1976; Aries, 1996). High-status and powerful individuals have been found to interrupt more often than low-status, less powerful individuals (West and Zimmerman, 1977). When individuals of low power status (females, persons of color) interact with individuals of high power status (males, whites), they tend to defer, please, notice, and attend to others' needs; speak tentatively and indirectly; be non-threatening; and make others comfortable (Wood and Dindia, 1998). In his study of a North Carolina courtroom, O'Barr (1981) observed that the use of some linguistic forms varied with the status and apparent social power of speakers, noting that low-status speakers tended to use "powerless speech" commonly associated with women's language styles, which Mulac (1998) identifies as hedges, intensifiers, tag questions, declaratives, rising intonations, polite forms, and hesitations—whereas high-status speakers tended to avoid these forms.

It is important to note that stereotype effects are evoked to a different degree depending on the situational context and are more pronounced when they are a salient issue in an interaction. For example, stereotypes have a larger impact in shaping expectations and perceptions in initial encounters, when more personal information about participants is not yet available (Aries, 1996).

Reexamination of Classroom Incivility from a Multicultural Perspective

Although Boice (1996) implicitly addresses cultural implications through his use of the subjective voice and language, anecdotal information, and personal reflections, an explicit discussion about the role that cultural perceptions play in influencing the degree of teacher-student interaction is sorely lacking and much needed. Since the study embodies the cultural orientations of a white male, its recommendations for curbing incidents of classroom incivility may not necessarily be as helpful to female faculty and faculty of color.

Erickson (2003) states: "Since our subjective world or perspectives— what we see, know, and want—[are] culturally constructed, and since culture varies, persons really do not inhabit the same subjective worlds" (p. 38). In other words, Erickson explicitly states what Boice (1996) merely implied. Tusmith and Reddy (2003) reinforce Erickson's view that culture determines subjectivity: "The position of the observer partially determines the context and quality of any observation" (p. 90). Therefore, we must explore the indirect influence that cultural perceptions, defined by stereotypes and social power, may have in fostering classroom incivility.

Cultural Perceptions Influence Classroom Dynamics. Individuals have multiple cultural identities—age, race, ethnicity, social class, sexual orientation—that differentiate them from other individuals. These cultural identities affect self-definition and patterns of interaction. Thus, the perception of an individual's behavior by self and others is influenced by the group membership of the person performing it.

In Boice's research (1996), teachers and students identified several kinds of classroom incivility as strongly disturbing. Two of these will be discussed as illustrating the role that cultural perceptions play in understanding classroom incivility.

1. Students conversing so loudly that lectures and student discussants could not be heard throughout a third or more of class meetings. A representative comment about this classroom incivility from students: "I don't understand this. Why doesn't she just tell some of the guys to shut up? Who's in charge?"

2. The presence of one or two "classroom terrorists" whose unpredictable and highly emotional outbursts (usually in the form of insulting complaints or intimidating disagreements) made the entire class tense. A representative comment about this classroom incivility from students: "Whew, it is unreal? She, all by herself, is screwing up everything. Everything. She talks all the time. She gets out of control, I think. She attacks anyone else who argues with her. I feel sort of, how can I say it, frightened by her."

Clearly, these disturbances reflect power struggles between students and the teacher. What is not clear, however, is the degree to which classroom incivility is the result of the teacher's deficit in immediacy behaviors, students' discomfort and unease with the subject material, students' hostility toward their teacher, or a combination of the three. What we do know is that how students evaluate their teachers' competence, credibility, and authority reflects the students' cultural perceptions.

Cultural Perceptions Affect Student Power and Teacher Immediacies. Tusmith and Reddy (2003) quote a teacher saying, "The racial/ethnic and gender factors that visibly identified me challenged my students' perceptions of how a professor should appear and act. The dual and contradictory position I embodied as native informant and authority figure was difficult for all of us in the classroom to negotiate" (p. 191).

Boice (1996) noted that how teachers present themselves may be the most telling factor, at least in initiating classroom incivility. The process of presentation centers on both students and their teacher, with each assessing the other in the context of cultural perceptions. Whether consciously or unconsciously, students will begin to engage in undermining behaviors (such as folding arms across the chest, slumped posture in the chair) prior to or upon the initial introduction of their teacher (such as when the teacher enters the classroom). Regardless of whether the teacher has employed prosocial or antisocial behaviors, some students begin to formulate their perceptions of their teacher's competence, authority, and personable characteristics prior to attending the first class. Perceptions are based either on what students have heard from their peers or on one or more of the teacher's known attributes (for example, if the teacher is an Asian American woman, she may be expected to be docile, compliant, accommodating, and employ indirect language style). These perceptions then become the student's expectations of the teacher. The extent of the students' undermining behavior will lessen or intensify depending on whether the teacher's behaviors are in accordance to students' own cultural expectations. Therefore, lessening classroom incivility may not simply involve the teacher employing more prosocial motivators and greater immediacy, but may also involve students readjusting their cultural perceptions and expectations within the social context.

Students' Roles in Perceptions of Classroom Incivility. On the surface, the first representative comment ("I don't understand this. Why doesn't she just tell some of the guys to shut up?") reflects a student's frustration with an instructor who would allow some of the students to disrupt class with their excessive talking. The student who made the comment perceives the instructor as lacking authority and legitimacy and as being powerless, prompting the question, "Who's in charge?" This type of comment raises a number of questions for consideration. What role, if any, does gender have in this manifestation of classroom incivility? What does it mean that the instructor is a she and not a he? What are the cultural implications when the student refers to the rude ones as "the guys"? Is the student referring to males or simply using "guys" as a general form to refer to a group of students? What would that term mean if the student making the comment were female? How does the student's cultural identity affect her perceptions of her teacher's competence and the place of "those guys" within the classroom setting? If we add some missing pieces, such as that the teacher is Asian American and the student who made the comment is a white male, what are the possible cultural perceptions this student may have in relation to his instructor and his assessment of who's in charge? And how might these perceptions affect the classroom dynamic? What immediacy behaviors might exacerbate or mitigate classroom incivility in this case?

The second representative comment, too, seems benign on the surface ("She talks all the time. She gets out of control, I think. She attacks anyone else who argues with her. I feel sort of. . . . frightened by her."). However, let's examine the student's comments from a cultural perspective. Let's say the student making the comment is a white female and the student she is describing is a black female. Given what the research has shown about the stereotypes associated with gender and racial or ethnic speech patterns and group behaviors, how are the cultural perceptions shaping the interactions of the "terrorist"—in this case a black female—with the white female? Is the black student really "out of control" or is her outspokenness being misinterpreted? What is it about the black student that makes her "frightening" to her classmate? And if we were to ask the black student about her classroom behavior, would she view her contributions to class discussions as so "aggressive, dominating, and hostile" that her classmate should be frightened by her? In this social context, who wields the power—the black female "terrorist" or the white student criticizing her?

Faculty Role in Classroom Incivility. Teaching as a faculty person of color at a predominately white institution, I have realized that it is not my scholarship but my very body that students learn from in the classroom; I am marked, as Tusmith (2003) points out, not only by my professional credentials but also by my race, age, and gender.

According to Kearney and Plax (1987), power in the classroom is relational, reflecting a power struggle between students and their teacher. Unlike their male and white colleagues, female faculty and faculty of color are cognizant of how their cultural identities complicate classroom dynamics, affecting the teaching situation. From the moment female faculty and faculty of color enter cultural space that is not of their own, they know they will be met with skepticism and that their credibility and authority will be called to question repeatedly throughout the term. They expect to meet some degree of classroom incivility simply because of who they are and what they represent. The insulting complaints and intimidating disagreements projected by students to their teachers often reflect students' discomfort with any subject material being delivered to them from a member of a subordinate group. The interaction may question students' cultural authority and their power of authority such that students of the dominant culture feel deficient. For example, the behaviors of a teacher who is an African American male to a predominately white audience will be interpreted differently from those of his white male colleague teaching the same subject material to a class of mostly whites. The white teacher's aggressive prodding may be perceived by the students as intellectually challenging, while the same behavior by the African American teacher may be perceived as hostile and argumentative.

The class dynamics and the cultural baggage students carry with them will determine the intensity of the classroom incivility female faculty and faculty of color experience. Many of the traumatic experiences cited by Boice (1996) can be seen in the light of Tusmith's comment (2003) that they are the "educational and professional consequences resulting from students' feelings of dissonance and disequilibrium when they are required to situate [female faculty and faculty] of color comfortably within their conceptions of power, intellect, and knowledge" (p. 287). For female faculty and faculty of color, classroom incivility is far from Boice's "mere problem of uninvolvement" (p. 464); it is a part of the teaching experience.

Strategies for Mitigating Classroom Incivility

Tusmith (2003) states, "There is an understanding of the hierarchy of authority—white professors face fewer direct challenges than do professors of color, whatever the course context. That lower level of hostility and challenge translate into a classroom environment in which it is easier for the professor's ability to maintain the class' respectful attention" (p. 110).

For faculty, particularly female faculty and faculty of color, teachers' referent and expert power have been found to be positively associated with student affect toward the teacher and the course material (Richmond, 1990; Richmond and McCroskey, 1984). Referent power is based on the students' ability to identify with the teacher and is operative only after the student and teacher have developed a relationship (Barraclough and Stewart, 1992). Thus, the teacher's referent power not only may gain compliance from students, but it also serves to build a trusting, open, positive teacher-student relationship (Richmond and Roach, 1992). For example, a white male teacher instructing a multicultural course to a class with few students of color may not only find it difficult to establish expertise, authority, and credibility with the non-white students, but he may also find it difficult to develop a rapport that would keep the levels of "terrorist" activity by the non-white students to a minimum or non-existent. In this social context it is paramount that the instructor be aware of how communication styles affect students' interpretation of the teacher's immediacy behaviors. Rather than responding dispassionately, such as moving away from the student discussion and thereby distancing himself or herself, the teacher should become more engaged in the discussion, rechanneling the student energy to greater inform the subject of discourse.

Power, privilege, and influence are all conveyed and perpetuated through interpersonal communication (Popp, Donovan, Marsh, and Peele, 2003). For example, an Asian non-native female speaking to a largely white male audience will be better received if she were to engage in language style that demonstrates strength, confidence, knowledge, and authority and to stay away from the powerless forms of language described earlier. Thus, it could be hypothesized that a powerful teacher is attuned to the classroom dynamic or teaching situation and employs immediacy behaviors such that all participants feel valued and empowered.

As Golish and Olson (2000) point out, "The less powerful students perceive their teacher, the more likely they will engage in undermining behavior because the professor lacks credibility. [Conversely,] the more powerful the instructor, the more power students feel because they respect the instructor and know that he or she will listen to their concerns" (p. 293). The key is in who wields the power. For female faculty and faculty of color, students initially wield the power, as their cultural perceptions will define their expectations of the teacher. How well the teacher meets students' expectations will inform how they assess the teacher's competency, credibility, and authority within the cultural norms. In other words, faculty are being evaluated on the basis of the subordinate cultural norms within the subtext of the dominant culture. Therefore, faculty, particularly female faculty and faculty of color, must first be deemed as having expertise and authority within the white culture before they can begin to change students' own cultural stereotypes and misperceptions of the subordinate group of which the teacher is a member. For example, the first day of class should be a time for the teacher to tell the students about his or her background in order to convey to students the teacher's expertise and authority. In addition, faculty should engage students by encouraging them to reveal information about themselves. This exercise will legitimize the teacher while providing a basis for teacher and student to develop rapport. In addition, the teacher must constantly assess the classroom climate and recognize that cultural perceptions defined by stereotypes will influence the level of intimacy between and among students and the teacher.

Mitigating classroom incivility is not simply the employment of more prosocial motivators and greater displays of immediacy by the teacher; rather, it is a by-product of how the teacher and student assess the sociocultural dynamics manifested in the classroom and how the teacher adapts his or her immediacy skills accordingly.

Conclusion

It seems that female faculty and faculty of color are more prone to experience greater levels of classroom incivility than their white, male colleagues in similar social contexts. Cultural perceptions, shaped by stereotypes and social power, are reflected in social interaction and seem to have an indirect influence on classroom incivility. It seems that the mitigating of classroom incivility involves more than increased teacher immediacies as suggested by Boice (1996).

References

Alfie, K. "Girl Talk, Guy Talk: Do Men and Women Really Have Distinctive Conversational Styles?" *Psychology Today,* Feb. 1988, 22.

Aries, E. *Men and Women in Interaction: Reconsidering the Differences.* New York: Oxford University Press, 1996.

Banks, J. "Multicultural Education: Characteristics and Goals." In J. Banks and C. M. Banks (eds.), *Multicultural Education: Issues and Perspectives.* (4th ed.) New York: Wiley, 2003.

Barraclough, R. A., and Stewart, R. A. "Power and Control: Social Science Perspectives." In V. P. Richmond and J. C. McCroskey (eds.), *Power in the Classroom: Communication, Control, and Concern.* Hillsdale: Erlbaum, 1992.

Boice, R. "Classroom Incivilities." *Research in Higher Education,* 1996, 37(4), 453–485.

Crawford, M. "Gender and Language." In R. Unger (ed.), *Handbook of the Psychology of Women and Gender.* New York: Wiley, 2001.

Edelsky, C. "Subjective Reactions to Sex-Linked Language." *Journal of Social Psychology,* 1976, 99, 97–104.

Erickson, F. "Culture in Society and in Educational Practice." In J. Banks and C. M. Banks (eds.), *Multicultural Education: Issues and Perspectives.* (4th ed.) New York: Wiley, 2003.

Golish, T., and Olson, L. "Students' Use of Power in the Classroom: An Investigation of Student Power, Teacher Power, and Teacher Immediacy." *Communication Quarterly,* 2000, 48(3), 293+.

Hart, A. and Morry, M. "Trait Inferences Based on Racial and Behavioral Cues." *Basic and Applied Social Psychology*, 1997, *19*(1), 33+.

Kearney, P., and Plax, T. "Situational and Individual Determinants of Teachers' Reported Use of Behavior Alteration Techniques." *Human Communication Research*, 1987, *14*, 145–166.

Kramarae, C. *Women and Men Speaking.* Boston: Newbury House, 1981.

Lakoff, R. "Language in Woman's Place." *Language in Society*, 1973, *2*, 45–79.

Mulac, A. "The Gender-Linked Language Effect: Do Language Differences Really Make a Difference?" In D. J. Canary and K. Dindia (eds.), *Sex Differences and Similarities in Communication: Critical Essays and Empirical Investigations of Sex and Gender in Interaction.* Hillsdale, N.J.: Erlbaum, 1998.

O'Barr, W. M. *Linguistic Evidence: Language, Power, and Strategy in the Courtroom.* Orlando: Academic Press, 1981.

Popp, D., Donovan, R., Marsh, K., and Peele, M. "Gender, Race, and Speech Style Stereotypes." *Sex Roles: A Journal of Research*, 2003, pp. 317+.

Richmond, V. P. "Communication in the Classroom: Power and Motivation." *Communication Education*, 1990, *39*, 181–195.

Richmond, V. P., and McCroskey, J. C. "Power in the Classroom II: Power and Learning." *Communication Education*, 1984, *33*, 125–136.

Richmond, V. P., and Roach, K. D. "Power in the Classroom: Seminal Studies." In V. P. Richmond and J. C. McCroskey (eds.), *Power in the Classroom: Communication, Control, and Concern.* Hillsdale, N.J.: Erlbaum, 1992.

Schofield, J. "The Colorblind Perspective in School: Causes and Consequences." In J. Banks and C. M. Banks (eds.), *Multicultural Education: Issues and Perspectives.* (4th ed.) New York: Wiley, 2003.

Siegler, D. M., and Siegler, R. S. "Stereotypes of Males' and Females' Speech." *Psychological Reports*, 1976, *39*, 167–170.

Tannen, D. *You Just Don't Understand.* New York: Ballantine, 1990.

Tatum, B. *Why Are All the Black Kids Sitting Together in the Cafeteria?: And Other Conversations About Race.* New York: Basic Books, 1997.

Tusmith, B., and Reddy, M. (eds.). *Race in the College Classroom: Pedagogy and Politics.* New Brunswick, N.J.: Rutgers University Press, 2003.

West, C., and Zimmerman, D. H. "Women's Place in Everyday Talk: Reflections on Parent-Child Interaction." *Social Problems*, 1977, *24*, 521–529.

Wood, J. T., and Dindia, K. "What's the Difference? A Dialogue About Differences and Similarities Between Women and Men." In D. J. Canary and K. Dindia (eds.), *Sex Differences and Similarities in Communication.* Mahwah, N.J.: Erlbaum, 1998.

MIA ALEXANDER-SNOW earned her Ph.D. in education and human development from Vanderbilt University and conducts research about the socialization of faculty of color at traditionally white colleges and universities.

PART TWO

Faculty Improprieties and Remedies

This chapter reports the results of research into how frequently students perceive faculty to engage in classroom improprieties and what they tend to do about it.

Incidence and Student Response to Faculty Teaching Norm Violations

John M. Braxton, Melinda Rogers Mann

A normative structure for undergraduate college teaching guides the professional choices of college and university faculty members to assure safeguarding the welfare of students as clients (Braxton and Bayer, 1999). Norms function as such a guide because they prescribe and proscribe patterns of behavior (Merton, 1973). Teaching misconduct in higher education occurs when faculty members violate those norms that govern undergraduate teaching role performance.

Norms and behavior are never perfectly correlated (Merton, 1976; Zuckerman, 1988). Merton (1976) elaborates by labeling this disjuncture a "painful contrast" between normative expectations for behavior and actual behavior (p. 40). Although the rate of teaching misconduct is unknown, we can expect violations of teaching norms to occur. An unknown rate of teaching misconduct leads to the perception that such improprieties are a rare event (Braxton and Bayer, 1999). Regarding teaching misconduct as a rare occurrence leads to the view that such wrongdoing bears little consequence to students. However, research shows that some harm to the welfare of students as clients of teaching results from teaching improprieties (see Chapter Five of this volume). Consequently, we need some knowledge of the frequency of teaching norm violations by college and university faculty members.

The normative structure of undergraduate college teaching empirically delineated by Braxton and Bayer (1999) consists of two categories of normative orientations: inviolable and admonitory norms. Inviolable norms include behaviors that faculty members believe should receive a severe sanction, whereas admonitory norms receive faculty disapproval, but an uncertain response (Braxton and Bayer, 1999). Because inviolable norms invoke greater disapproval from college and university faculty members, we focus in this chapter on student perceptions of the frequency of inviolable teaching norm violations.

In light of the potential harm to students, the social control of teaching wrongdoing takes on critical importance. The mechanisms of social control include the deterrence, detection, and sanctioning of wrongdoing (Zuckerman, 1977, 1988). Although individual faculty members, department chairpersons, and academic affairs officers play a role in these mechanisms of social control, undergraduate college students bear the primary responsibility for detecting teaching misconduct by faculty members, given that they directly observe faculty teaching behaviors (Braxton, Bayer, and Noseworthy, 2002). The sanctioning of teaching wrongdoing depends on the actions of students who personally observe faculty members violating teaching norms.

However, as Braxton, Bayer, and Noseworthy (2002) point out, undergraduate students may play a weak role in the detection of teaching misconduct. They observe that students espouse a lower level of disapproval for the proscriptive behaviors of the normative structure for undergraduate college teaching than do college and university faculty members, making detection and reporting of faculty teaching norm violations by students seem problematic. These assumptions, however, are an open empirical question. Knowledge of the types of actions taken by students for personally observed incidents of inviolable norm violations may shed light on the role students play in detecting and reporting teaching misconduct.

Thus, we concentrate on the actions students take for personally observed incidents of inviolable teaching norm violations. The research on which this report is based—the *National Assessment of College Student Classroom Experience Survey* (the *Survey*) for the academic year 1999–2000—is described in the Appendix of this volume. The means are based on responses from a sample of 4,200 undergraduates.

Faculty Norm Violations

Of the seven inviolable norms delineated by Braxton and Bayer (1999), six are observable by students and are included in this study. They include condescending negativism, inattentive planning, moral turpitude, particularistic grading, personal disregard, and uncommunicated course details. These six norms are described in Table A.1 of the Appendix.

We measured the frequency of violations of these six norms using the perceptions of students. For each of the teaching behaviors observable to students that reflect one of the six inviolable normative patterns included on the *Survey,* survey respondents were asked how frequently they had observed such behavior in their classes during the current academic year (1999–2000). A four-point response scale was provided: 0 = Never, 1 =

Table 4.1. Student Observations of Faculty Teaching Norm Violations

Inviolable Norms Observable by Students	Percentage responding "never observed" (0.0)	Percentage responding "rarely observed" (0.10 to 1.49)	Percentage responding "sometimes observed" (1.50 or higher)
Condescending negativism	18.9%	75.6%	5.5%
Inattentive planning	28.6	51.8	19.6
Moral turpitude	79.8	18.4	1.8
Particularistic grading	21.5	73.3	5.3
Personal disregard	9.4	87.6	3.0
Uncommunicated course details	43.6	53.5	2.9

Note: Categories 2 ("occasionally") and 3 ("frequently") were combined in the table due to lower response totals in those categories. The combined results are in the "sometimes observed" column.

Rarely, 2 = Occasionally, and 3 = Frequently. The frequencies with which students reported observing the various norm violations are shown in Table 4.1.

Frequency of Norm Violations

Several observations emerge from Table 4.1. The vast majority of students recounted that they never or rarely observed faculty infractions of these norms during the 1999–2000 academic year at their college or university. However, breaches of the norm of inattentive planning tended to occur the most frequently, as 19.6 percent of respondents reported that they sometimes observed faculty members behaving in such a way. Also, about 5 percent of student respondents reported observing violations of the norms of condescending negativism and particularistic grading during the current academic year. At the other extreme, the overwhelming majority (79.8 percent) of students reported that they never observed violations of the norm of moral turpitude during the 1999–2000 academic year, and less than 2 percent (1.8 percent) of respondents indicate that they sometimes observed faculty members violating this norm.

Actions by Students in Response to Norm Violations

We identified the actions taken by undergraduate college students for personally observed incidents of teaching misconduct through their written responses to the following question appearing on the *Survey:* "If you have observed any incidents of what you might consider as classroom misconduct—by either students or faculty members—please describe the most grievous one, and what if anything you did in response." Of the 831 students who completed the *Survey,* 164 students responded to this open-ended question.

We reviewed these 164 responses to see if any of the incidents of faculty classroom misconduct deemed as most grievous by students correspond to those proscribed behaviors reflective of one of the six inviolable norms. We classified thirty of these most grievous incidents as a violation of either the norm of condescending negativism (eight responses), personal disregard (twelve responses), particularistic grading (four responses), moral turpitude (four responses) or the norm of uncommunicated course details (three responses). Each of these thirty responses also registers the type of action taken in response to the incident described.

The actions taken by undergraduate college students range from doing nothing to direct formal action. No action was reported by seven students, whereas eleven students report taking such direct formal action as reporting the incident to a dean or a department chairperson. Another six students reported that they talked directly with the offending faculty member about the incident. The remaining seven students describe taking indirect action toward the offending faculty member in the form of dropping the course, reporting the incident on the course evaluation form, leaving the class immediately after the incident, or leaving school.

To sum up, less than 25 percent of students observing a teaching norm violation reported doing nothing. In contrast, more than half (seventeen out of thirty) of such students described taking direct action either by talking to the offending faculty member or by reporting the incident to a dean or department chairperson at their institution.

Conclusions

As Hackett (1999) reports, the lay public demonstrated a willingness to exercise social control for research misconduct following some well-publicized cases of scientific misconduct. Congressional action in response to these cases led to the establishment of the Office of Inspector General of the National Science Foundation (NSF) and the Office of Research Integrity of the National Institutes of Health (NIH) (LaFollette, 1999). These offices investigate and sanction incidents of scientific wrongdoing.

Such exercise of formal social control by the lay public raises a question concerning the rate of scientific wrongdoing. Swazey, Anderson, and Louis (1993) estimate that between 6 percent and 9 percent of faculty and students have directly observed research misconduct. At the other extreme, a survey conducted by the Office of the Inspector General of NSF discerned that 20 percent of scientists are aware of cases of fraud, a severe form of scientific misconduct (1990).

If we use the response category of "sometimes observed" exhibited in Table 4.1, we conclude that 5 percent to 19 percent of undergraduate students in our sample observed faculty violating the teaching norms of condescending negativism, inattentive planning, and particularistic grading during the 1999–2000 academic year. Violations of these three norms approximate the 6 percent to 9 percent rates of scientific misconduct identified by

Swazey, Anderson, and Louis (1993). However, violations of the norms of moral turpitude, personal disregard, and uncommunicated course details fall below the estimated rate of scientific wrongdoing.

The lay public expects little or no scientific malfeasance. Since the lay public views undergraduate teaching as the most important responsibility of college and university faculty members (Ewell, 1994), we assert that the lay public also demands that there be little or no teaching misconduct and will not tolerate it. Consequently, colleges and universities must embrace an attentive stance toward responding to faculty teaching norm violations through detecting and responding to such violations.

Moreover, Braxton, Bayer, and Noseworthy (2002) suggest that students may play a weak role in the social control of teaching misconduct. In stark contrast to this assertion, our findings lead us to conclude that students tend to wield strong social control when they witness a norm violation that they judge as most grievous. Such strong social control takes the form of either talking to the offending faculty member or of reporting the incident to a dean or department chairperson.

Recommendations for Practice

The conclusions presented above indicate that the lay public must perceive that colleges and universities in general and faculty members in particular take seriously their responsibility to safeguard the welfare of students as clients of teaching role performance. In exchange, the lay public grants autonomy for teaching role performance to members of the professoriate (Braxton and Bayer, 1999; Goode, 1969). Moreover, students who witness teaching misconduct show a willingness to take direct action by either talking to the offending faculty member or by reporting the incident to a department chairperson or a dean. Recommendations for just such action are found in Chapter Six of this volume.

Final Thoughts

The findings of this study suggest that teaching norm violations are neither rampant nor non-existent. Nevertheless, the social control of such violations must occur to protect the welfare of undergraduate students as clients of teaching role performance. Accordingly, undergraduate students, individual faculty members, department chairpersons, and deans should shoulder some responsibility for detecting and addressing teaching norm violations. The enactment of the six recommendations for policy and practice detailed in Chapter Six would demonstrate an acceptance of this responsibility. Moreover, the implementation of these recommendations would assure the lay public that student welfare is of critical importance. Such assurance, in turn, would serve to preserve the autonomy for teaching role performance granted by the lay public to members of the professoriate.

References

Braxton, J. M., and Bayer, A. E. *Faculty Misconduct in Collegiate Teaching.* Baltimore: Johns Hopkins University Press, 1999.

Braxton, J. M., Bayer, A. E., and Noseworthy, J. A. "Students as Tenuous Agents of Social Control of Professorial Misconduct." *Peabody Journal of Education,* 2002, 77, 101–124.

Carnegie Foundation for the Advancement of Teaching. *A Classification of Institutions of Higher Education.* Princeton: Princeton University Press, 1999.

Ewell, P. T. "The Neglected Art of Collective Responsibility: Restoring Our Links with Society." Paper commissioned for the American Association of Higher Education Forum on Faculty Roles and Rewards Second National Conference, New Orleans, 1994.

Goode, W. J. "The Theoretical Limits of Professionalization." In A. Etzioni (ed.), *The Semi-Professions and Their Organization.* New York: Free Press, 1969.

Goode, W. J., and Hatt, P. K. *Methods of Social Research.* New York: McGraw-Hill, 1952.

Hackett, E. J. "A Social Control Perspective on Scientific Misconduct." In J. M. Braxton (ed.), *Perspectives on Scholarly Misconduct in the Sciences.* Columbus: Ohio State University Press, 1999.

LaFollette, M. C. "A Foundation of Trust: Scientific Misconduct." In J. M. Braxton (ed.), *Perspectives on Scholarly Misconduct in the Sciences.* Columbus: Ohio State University Press, 1999.

Merton, R. K. *The Sociology of Science: Theoretical and Empirical Investigations.* Chicago: University of Chicago Press, 1973.

Merton, R. K. "The Sociology of Social Problems." In R. K. Merton and R. Nisbet (eds.), *Contemporary Social Problems.* Orlando: Harcourt Brace, 1976.

Office of Inspector General. *Survey Data on the Extent of Misconduct in Science and Engineering.* Washington, D.C.: National Science Foundation, 1990.

Swazey, J. P., Anderson, M. S., and Louis, K. S. "Ethical Problems in Academic Research." *American Scientist,* 1993, 81, 542–553.

Zuckerman, H. E. "Deviant Behavior and Social Control in Science." In E. Sagarin (ed.), *Deviance and Social Change.* Thousand Oaks, Calif.: Sage, 1977.

Zuckerman, H. E. "The Sociology of Science." In N. J. Smelser (ed.), *Handbook of Sociology.* Thousand Oaks, Calif.: Sage, 1988.

JOHN M. BRAXTON is professor of education in the Higher Education Leadership and Policy Program, Peabody College, Vanderbilt University.

MELINDA ROGERS MANN is a doctoral student in the Higher Education Leadership and Policy Program, Peabody College, Vanderbilt University.

5

When the instructor violates the norms of teaching, there is an impact on student learning.

The Influence of Teaching Norm Violations on the Welfare of Students as Clients of College Teaching

John M. Braxton, Alan E. Bayer, James A. Noseworthy

As Goode (1969) has noted, the ideal of service constitutes one of the key generating traits of a profession. The ideal of service embodies a commitment of members of a profession to the welfare of its clients. Put differently, Goode notes, the welfare of the clients and their best interests determine the choices made by the individual professional.

College students as individuals and as a class make up the core group of clients related to faculty teaching role performance (Braxton and Bayer, 1999). College and university faculty members make a range of professional choices in their day-to-day teaching role performance that affect the welfare of students as clients. Such choices involve planning their courses, communicating with students in their classes, developing grading criteria for student assignments and examinations, interacting with students in class, and various decisions about course content (Braxton, Bayer, and Noseworthy, 2002).

Moreover, most college and university faculty members possess considerable autonomy in making choices regarding these aspects of teaching role performance (Braxton and Bayer, 1999; Braxton, Bayer, and Noseworthy, 2002). As a consequence of such autonomy, norms—as prescriptive and proscriptive patterns of behavior (Merton, 1973)—must exist to safeguard the welfare of students. Without norms, faculty members are free to make unconstrained and idiosyncratic choices in the performance of their teaching role (Braxton, Bayer, and Noseworthy, 2002).

NEW DIRECTIONS FOR TEACHING AND LEARNING, no. 99, Fall 2004 © Wiley Periodicals, Inc.

An empirically derived normative structure for undergraduate college teaching exists. Braxton and Bayer (1999) describe this normative structure as comprised of what they call inviolable norms and admonitory norms. Faculty members believe that some behavioral patterns warrant severe sanctions. Such norms are labeled as inviolable. Other behavioral patterns invoke disapproval but with an uncertain sanctioning response. Such norms are called admonitory. In the present study, we employ a subset of these previously identified norms. This subset includes all of the previously identified norms that meet two criteria: (1) they involve behaviors that would normally be directly observable by students and are directed to the student as client, and (2) they meet standards or assumptions required for robust statistical analyses.

A critically important assumption undergirds this normative structure for undergraduate college teaching: faculty adherence to inviolable and admonitory norms that are pertinent to students safeguards students' welfare and serves their best interests (Braxton and Bayer, 1999). Put differently, we assume that faculty violations of these norms adversely affect students. This important assumption warrants empirical testing. Consequently, this chapter presents the findings of research conducted to determine the effects of violations of those inviolable and admonitory norms applicable to students as clients of teaching role performance on the welfare of students. Student perceptions of violations of these norms provide the basis for this piece of research. (The research on which this chapter is based is described in this volume's Appendix.)

Conceptual Framework

Aspects of the welfare of students safeguarded by adherence to the norms of undergraduate college teaching include student learning of course content, their development of cognitive skills, and their future careers. Poor course planning, deficient course design, and inadequate communication with a class lead to students failing to keep up with the readings of their courses and to finish graded assignments (Braxton and Bayer, 1999). Inadequate faculty preparation for a course may also harm student course learning. Moreover, faulty course planning by faculty members negatively affects the development of student cognitive skills (Pascarella and others, 1996; Edison, Doyle, and Pascarella, 1998).

The inviolable norms of inattentive planning and uncommunicated course details and the admonitory norms of inadequate communication, inadequate course design, and insufficient syllabus delineated by Braxton and Bayer (1999) and defined in the Appendix's Table A.1 proscribe such behaviors. To elaborate, the norm focusing on inattentive planning rebukes the lack of attention to planning a course, whereas the norm focusing on uncommunicated course details criticizes a faculty member's failure to inform students of important particulars about a course on the first day of class. The norm focusing on inadequate communication pertains to a faculty member's failure to convey course details to students; the norm focusing on inadequate course design rejects poor preparation for teaching a course; and insufficient syllabus deems as inappropriate a faculty member's failure to provide students with an adequate syllabus for a course. Thus, faculty violations of the *proscriptive* norms of inattentive planning, inadequate course design, insufficient syllabus, uncommunicated course details, and inadequate communication harm students' learning of course content and developing cognitive skills. Conversely, faculty conformity to the corresponding *prescriptive* norms fosters student course learning and their development of cognitive skills.

Faculty violations of the proscriptive norms of condescending negativism and personal disregard negatively affect the climate of a college classroom. Treating students in a demeaning and condescending manner (condescending negativism) or showing disrespect for the needs and sensitivities of students (personal disregard) lead to a classroom climate marked by strain and disharmony (Braxton and Bayer, 1999). In contrast, faculty members who follow the corresponding positive versions of these norms create a classroom climate marked by harmony and openness.

Students' course learning, students' development of cognitive skills, and their future careers depend to some extent on the grading of course assignments on the basis of merit (Braxton and Bayer, 1999). Merit-based grading produces unbiased estimates of student course learning. Future performance in other undergraduate courses, academic performance in graduate school, and performance in one's future career also depend on grades that are unbiased estimates of student course learning. Thus, harm to students results from faculty violations of the proscriptive norm of particularistic grading, such as uneven or preferential treatment of students in the awarding of grades.

These formulations suggest the following hypothesis: Faculty violations of the proscriptive norms of inattentive planning, inadequate course design, insufficient syllabus, uncommunicated course details, inadequate communication, condescending negativism, personal disregard, and particularistic grading negatively affect the academic and intellectual development of undergraduate college students.

To test these hypotheses, we gathered student assessments of their own academic and intellectual development, which we assert provide an index of the extent to which the interests and welfare of students are served, and estimated the influence of each faculty norm violation on student perceptions of their academic and intellectual development above and beyond the influence of each of the five control variables through regression analysis. The details of the research and analyses are shown in the Appendix at the end of this volume.

Table 5.1. Means and Standard Deviations of Reported Frequencies of Proscriptive Teaching Norms

Description of Norm	Mean*	Standard Deviation
Inviolable Norms		
Violation of condescending negativism	.55	.52
Violation of inattentive planning	.73	.69
Violation of particularistic grading	.51	.50
Violation of personal disregard	.59	.44
Violation of uncommunicated course detail	.37	.48
Admonitory Norms		
Violation of inadequate communication	.73	.47
Violation of inadequate course design	1.59	1.05
Violation of insufficient syllabus	.71	.54

Note: *Scale 0–3; 0 = never, 3 = frequently.

Findings

Table 5.1 shows the means and standard deviations for each of the eight proscriptive teaching norms described earlier as reported by students. (Note that the norm of moral turpitude listed in Appendix Table A.1 is not included in these analyses for the statistical reasons described in the Appendix.)

When these data are analyzed using regression analysis (see Appendix Tables A.3, definitions of variables; A.4, inviolable norms; and A.5, admonitory norms), they support our hypothesis that faculty violations of each of the eight normative orientations of undergraduate college teaching negatively affect the academic and intellectual development of students above and beyond the influence of the five control variables. Put differently, inadequate faculty preparation for a course—poor course planning, deficient course design, inadequate communication—harms the academic and intellectual development of students. Faculty in-class interactions with students characterized by treating students in a condescending and demeaning way as well as being insensitive to their need for respect as individuals also adversely affect the academic and intellectual development of students. The grading of student examinations and papers based on criteria other than merit also hampers the academic and intellectual development of students. In stark contrast, faculty adherence to each of the eight normative patterns fosters the academic and intellectual development of students. Table A.1 in the Appendix shows the specific proscriptive behaviors that make up each of these eight normative patterns of undergraduate college teaching.

Conclusions and Recommendations for Practice

Although the findings of this study are provocative, the conclusions we draw from them must be viewed as provisional pending support from further research. We offer the following three conclusions:

1. Faculty adherence to each of the six inviolable and three admonitory norms applicable to students tends to safeguard their welfare as clients of undergraduate teaching role performance. Moreover, these normative orientations are social realities that protect the interests and welfare of students as clients.

2. In addition to safeguarding the welfare of students as clients, faculty faithfulness to these normative orientations also fosters the achievement of faculty teaching goals for undergraduate education. To elaborate, the academic and intellectual development of students parallels a cluster of goals that Liebert and Bayer (1975) call the development of basic intellectual functions. They classify such goals as *clear-thinking, creativity,* and *self-directed learning.*

3. Faculty members tend to accord only an admonitory level of sanction for behaviors that reflect the norms of inadequate communication, inadequate course design, and insufficient syllabus (Braxton and Bayer, 1999). However, the harm to the welfare of students as clients that occurs because of faculty violations of these norms suggests that these normative violations should also be viewed as severe pedagogical infractions. These three normative orientations pertain to the competent and responsible planning of courses by faculty members.

We also believe that this interpretation offers suggestions for institutional practices that would protect the rights of students. These are detailed in the next chapter.

References

Braxton, J. M., and Bayer, A. E. *Faculty Misconduct in Collegiate Teaching.* Baltimore: Johns Hopkins University Press, 1999.

Braxton, J. M., Bayer, A. E., and Noseworthy, J. A. "Students as Tenuous Agents of Social Control of Professorial Misconduct." *Peabody Journal of Education,* 2002, 77, 101–124.

Edison, M., Doyle, S., and Pascarella, E. T. "Dimensions of Teaching Effectiveness and Their Impact on Student Cognitive Development." Paper presented at the annual meeting of the Association for the Study of Higher Education, Miami, 1998.

Goode, W. J. "The Theoretical Limits of Professionalization." In A. Etzioni (ed)., *The Semi-Professions and Their Organization.* New York: Free Press, 1969.

Liebert, R. J., and Bayer, A. E. "Goals in Teaching Undergraduates: Professional Reproduction and Client-Centeredness." *The American Sociologist,* 1975, 10, 195–205.

Merton, R. K. *The Sociology of Science: Theoretical and Empirical Investigations.* Chicago: University of Chicago Press, 1973.

Mulkay, M. "Norms and Ideology in Science." *Social Science Information,* 1976, 15, 637–656.

Pascarella, E. T., and others. "Effects of Teacher Organization/Preparation and Teacher Skill/Clarity on General Cognitive Skills in College." *Journal of College Student Development*, 1996, *35*, 7–19.

JOHN M. BRAXTON *is professor of education in the Higher Education Leadership and Policy Program, Peabody College, Vanderbilt University.*

ALAN E. BAYER *is professor of sociology, adjunct professor of science studies, and director of the Center for Survey Research at Virginia Polytechnic Institute and State University.*

JAMES A. NOSEWORTHY *is president of Hiwassee College, a United Methodist-related residential two-year college in Tennessee.*

6

Bringing together the results of the research reported in
Chapters Four and Five, this chapter provides
recommendations for instructor behavior consistent with
the best criteria for ethical behavior toward students.

Toward a Code of Conduct for Undergraduate Teaching

John M. Braxton, Alan E. Bayer

Professorial misconduct in the research realm has drawn considerable attention over the last several decades. Many professional associations have now adopted a code of conduct or a code of ethics that addresses proper and improper research practices. Individual academic institutions have established both policies addressing research improprieties and committees to deal with instances of deviation from these policies and codes of conduct.

In contrast, there is no parallel infrastructure to address professorial misconduct in the teaching role. Indeed, policies and practices on classroom incivility have been largely confined to addressing student behavior. However, Tabachnick, Keith-Spiegel, and Pope (1991) and Svinicki (1994) initiated reframing the focus by expressly addressing ethics in college teaching. The interplay between student incivility and professorial misconduct is suggested by Svinicki (1994) when she asserts that teachers' behavior models that expected of students. Boice (1996) broadened the discourse on campus incivilities by suggesting that a high proportion of student misconduct is prompted by professorial incivilities. Consequently, Decoo (2002), Hamilton (2002), and other contemporary observers of the academy have increasingly focused on improprieties in the teaching role.

In our book, *Faculty Misconduct in Collegiate Teaching* (1999), we address professorial misconduct in the teaching role and recommend that another means of addressing commensurate problems is through institutional establishment of a code of conduct in relation to teaching. Based on the survey results and empirical analyses reviewed in the current volume, we propose that institutions consider developing codes of conduct as a means to address faculty misconduct in collegiate teaching.

The expectation of self-regulation by professionals, as with the research enterprise several decades ago, is today found to be insufficient. College and university faculty members possess a great deal of autonomy as professionals in their roles as teachers and researchers. However, the value of the autonomy of professional workers does not supersede the expectations of self-regulation by professionals.

Faculty autonomy constitutes one of the defining values of the academic profession (Braxton and Bayer, 1999). As a consequence, faculty members generally believe that colleague or administrative interventions should be avoided in matters of teaching improprieties, except in the most grievous of instances. However, incidents of inappropriate behavior in the classroom and in teaching roles have eroded public trust and increased public skepticism of professorial conduct and demeanor.

This rise in public concern is partly accelerated by the loss in authority and respect bestowed upon the professoriate by students. Students, rather than colleagues or institutional administrators, are the primary observers of teaching role performance. Therefore, wrongdoing in teaching is highly visible by the student as client even if not by others and, in the context of increased student rights and decreased student deference to the professoriate, more likely to be conveyed to other faculty members, administrators, and parents and guardians. As a result, there is now greater public awareness and expectation that classroom improprieties need to be formally addressed.

The professional standards of faculty viewing students as clients, safeguarding the welfare of students as clients, and the general expectation of the ideal of service appear no longer to be sufficient professional expectations. Norms related to teaching now need to be articulated and adopted in codes of conduct, much as they have been with regard to research misconduct.

Unlike in the research field, the origin for establishing such codes lies more exclusively within the domain of the academic department and the academic institution. Similarly, the infrastructure for formal and informal sanctioning of behavior lies solely with the academic institution rather than being shared with professional associations and governmental agencies, as is the case in sanctioning research misconduct.

Hence we outline some of the fundamental requirements for professional codes of conduct in teaching and propose some key elements of such a code for academic institutions. Specifically, we focus on those behaviors relating to teaching that have direct impact on the student as client. There are normative violations within the teaching sphere that are not observable by students and thus affect them only indirectly. These include, among others, refusing a request by one's department to advise students, refusing to participate in departmental curricular planning, and failing to share course syllabi and successful teaching methods with colleagues. However, we focus here on those behaviors that impinge directly and adversely on the student as client.

The tenets of the code we propose serve as a foundation for elaboration by the individual collegiate institution or academic department. In devising the code we propose, we adhered to three essential elements. The first element is that each tenet of the code should safeguard the welfare of students as clients of undergraduate college teaching, with particular emphasis on their learning and personal development. Second, each tenet should be specific enough to permit observation of pertinent teaching behaviors by students and faculty colleagues. Third, for the code to be perceived as legitimate, each tenet should emanate from empirical research.

Informal norms or guides to appropriate or inappropriate behavior provide a basis for the development of the tenets of a formal code of conduct. In *Faculty Misconduct in Collegiate Teaching* (1999) we identify a normative structure for undergraduate college teaching. The norms that make up this structure safeguard the welfare of students as clients. The norms we identify spring from the perceptions of 949 faculty members from the full spectrum of colleges and universities (research universities, comprehensive colleges and universities, liberal arts colleges, and two-year colleges) and from a representative cross section of academic disciplines (biology, mathematics, history, and psychology). This empirically derived normative structure provides the cornerstone for the tenets of the code of conduct for undergraduate college teaching we set forth in this chapter.

Teaching activities such as course planning and course design, faculty communication with a class, grading criteria for student assignments and examinations, the treatment of course content, and relationships with students in a class present opportunities for improprieties by faculty members and, in some cases, graduate teaching assistants. The norms we empirically derived proscribe related inappropriate behaviors regarding these and other instructionally related activities. The code of conduct we propose stems from these possible improprieties. We strive to deter such improprieties by the advancement of a code of conduct for undergraduate college teaching.

A Code of Conduct for Undergraduate College Teaching

We advance ten tenets that institutional codes of conduct for undergraduate college teaching should include. The tenets are related to our empirical findings delineating clusters of proscriptive norms (shown in italic in the following discussion). Some additional norms included below are drawn from Baxton and Bayer (1999).

1. Undergraduate courses should be carefully planned. Textbooks and other course materials must be ordered in time to be available for use by enrolled students. An adequate course syllabus must also be prepared.

This principle springs from the normative patterns of *inattentive planning* and *insufficient syllabus* components of the normative structure we empirically identified. Inattentive planning rebukes faculty inattention to course planning. Insufficient syllabus proscribes the failure to provide an adequate syllabus to students enrolled in a course.

2. Important course details should be conveyed to enrolled students. Such details include office hours, policy on class attendance, changes in class meeting location or time, reading assignments, opportunities for extra credit, grading criteria for essay questions on examinations or papers, and the instructor's policy on missed or make-up examinations.

This tenet emanates from the proscriptive norms of *uncommunicated course details* and *inadequate communication.*

3. New and revised lectures and course readings should reflect advancements of knowledge in a field. This tenet stipulates that faculty members must keep up to date with advancements of knowledge in their academic disciplines.

The normative pattern of *inadequate course design* supplies the foundation for this tenet.

4. Grading of examinations and assignments should be based on merit and not on the characteristics of students. Personal friendships with students should not affect the grades given them. Moreover, no student should be given preferential treatment in the application of policies about late work and incompletes and opportunities for extra-credit work to improve their grades.

The foundation for this tenet is the norm of *particularistic grading* that we empirically delineated. This tenet finds reinforcement from ethical statements regarding college teaching (Svinicki, 1994).

5. Various perspectives on course topics should be presented, examinations should cover the breadth of the course, and scholars' or students' perspectives at variance with the instructor's point of view should be acknowledged.

The proscriptive norms of *authoritarian classroom* and *instructional narrowness* (Braxton and Bayer, 1999) provide the basis for this particular tenet. Authoritarian classroom and instructional narrowness reject a rigid and closed approach to course content and the insistence that students adhere to a particular perspective on course topics.

6. Students should be treated with respect as individuals. Students must not be treated in a condescending and demeaning way. The needs and sensitivities of students should be respected.

The norms of *condescending negativism* and *personal disregard* give rise to this tenet. Statements of ethical principles of college teaching resonate with these two norms (Svinicki, 1994).

7. Faculty members must respect the confidentiality of their relationships with students and the students' academic achievements.

This tenet springs from the norm of *inconvenience avoidance* (Braxton and Bayer, 1999). This normative orientation proscribes faculty attempts to avoid personal inconveniences due to the courses they teach. Such rebuked attempts to avoid being inconvenienced include returning graded papers and examinations by leaving them in a location where students can see the grades given to other students.

8. Faculty members must make themselves available to their students by maintaining office hours and being prepared for student advising, including being prepared to identify special services available for students with problems outside the expertise of the faculty member.

The proscriptive norm of *advisement negligence* (Braxton and Bayer, 1999) provides the basis for this tenet. Faculty have an instructionally related obligation to provide advising to students regarding their course and conscientious concern for student care beyond course subject matter.

9. Faculty members must not have sexual relationships with students enrolled in their classes. Faculty members must also refrain from making sexual comments to students.

10. Faculty members must not come to class intoxicated from alchohol or drugs.

The norm of *moral turpitude* provides the basis for the last two tenets of this proposed code of conduct. Moral turpitude chastises depraved, unprincipled behavior by faculty members.

We expect that individual colleges and universities will elaborate on the tenets we have put forth and develop additional ones. We urge that the development of additional tenets adhere to the three essential characteristics of codes of conduct previously discussed. To satisfy the need for an empirical grounding to a code of conduct, colleges and universities wishing to include additional tenets should conduct audits of the normative orientations held by their faculty members.

Implementing the Code of Conduct

Perceived legitimacy of a code of conduct by administrators, faculty, and students represents a critical element in the efficacy of such a code. The ratification of the code of conduct for undergraduate collegiate teaching by the institution's faculty senate or other faculty governing body constitutes an essential step in the implementation of an institutional code of conduct. The perceived legitimacy of such a code by faculty members depends on appropriate faculty approval. Approval by an institution's board of trustees also fosters the perceived legitimacy of such a code of conduct.

The following six recommendations for policy and practice, some of which were previously proposed in our book *Faculty Misconduct,* demonstrate an institutional and professorial commitment to protecting the welfare of students.

1. Individual colleges and universities should maintain official records of reported incidents of teaching misconduct.

The findings of this study buttress this recommendation. Such records should indicate whether an investigation of the reported incident took place and the outcome of the investigation.

2. Individual colleges and universities should form Teaching Integrity Committees.

The role of such a formal committee would be to consider reported incidents of teaching wrongdoing. The processes used by such a committee need to protect both the faculty member accused of offense and the individual reporting the incident. The processes of such a committee should also make it easy for undergraduate students to report incidents.

In cases where the teaching integrity committee finds that a tenet of the code of conduct has been violated, the committee should consider the degree of harm done by the code violation to the welfare of the student as a client of teaching. The pervasiveness of the impropriety by the offending faculty member or graduate teaching assistant should also be considered. In those cases where considerable harm occurred and the offending behavior represents a pervasive pattern of behavior, the Teaching Integrity Committee should recommend sanctions.

The range of sanctions that a Teaching Integrity Committee may recommend should be stated in the faculty manuals or handbooks of the college or university adopting a code of conduct. These sanctions may include the extreme sanction of terminating the offending faculty member or teaching assistant. Franke (2002) provides a helpful list of less severe actions. Colleges and universities committed to developing a code of conduct for undergraduate college teaching should consider the actions Franke suggests. Her list includes a warning or a reprimand, public censure, departmental transfer, no salary increase, reduction in salary, suspension, peer monitoring of the classes of the offending individual, and required counseling or workshop attendance. The sanction recommended should reflect the harm done and the frequency with which the offending individual engages in the tenet of the code violated. The more pervasive the behavior and the greater the harm done, the greater the severity of the sanction recommended.

3. Student course-rating instruments should include items that reflect the six teaching norms observable by students: condescending negativism, inattentive planning, personal disregard, particularistic grading, moral turpitude, and uncommunicated course details.

The inclusion of such items on student course-rating instruments gives students who prefer to take either no action or indirect action for personally observed incidents of teaching misconduct an opportunity to vent their concern over teaching norm violations labeled as most grievous. Frequent teaching norm violations by individual faculty members should carry a negative weight in decisions about annual salary increments, reappointment, tenure, and promotion.

4. Academic department chairpersons and deans—of both academic and student affairs—should include handling reported incidents of teaching wrongdoing as part of their administrative duties.

Chairpersons and deans should handle each reported incident in an open and fair manner. Students who report incidents should be taken seriously. A balance between protecting the student and the accused faculty member is of utmost importance. Chairs and deans may take informal action for some incidents, whereas the more egregious violations of teaching norms may require more formal action. A department chair may decide to establish an ad hoc committee to investigate such incidents. If a Teaching Integrity Committee exists, then a department chair or dean may refer such teaching norm violations to this committee for deliberation.

5. Academic departments should formulate policies and procedures to handle student concerns and complaints in general and those that pertain to teaching in particular.

Such policies and procedures should specify how students may register their concerns and complaints to the department chairperson. Reporting incidents of teaching norm violations should be made easy for students who wish to register their concerns. Such policies and procedures must protect students from retaliation by the accused faculty member. Confidentiality of the accusing student's identity should be strictly maintained if the student is enrolled in the accused faculty member's class.

6. Student handbooks should include brief descriptions of the six teaching norms observable by students as well as information on how students can report teaching misbehavior.

The student handbook should make it easy for students to find where they should go in order to report incidents, especially those that occur in classes held in other departments. Since students may find difficulty locating a department chair in a class taken outside of their major department, there should be one person or one office in student affairs listed in the student handbook that students may contact to report teaching misbehavior if they are unsure which department chair to approach. In addition, with clarification of the six types of teaching misconduct observable by students in the handbook, students can better understand the types of observable teaching misconduct that they should report as a part of their student rights and responsibilities.

Closing Thoughts

Administrators and faculty members at individual colleges and universities may question why their institution should develop a code of conduct for undergraduate college teaching. Many individuals may hold that teaching improprieties are a rare occurrence at their institution. If improprieties are rare, they question why a formal code of conduct is needed.

The promulgation of a code of conduct for undergraduate college teaching constitutes a proactive step by individual colleges and universities. Although our research demonstrates that a normative structure for undergraduate college teaching exists, norms and behaviors are never perfectly related. Put differently, norms do not prevent teaching improprieties. Consequently, codes of conduct for undergraduate college teaching should be developed by individual colleges and universities, or academic departments, before publicly known incidents of teaching misconduct occur at their institutions. Nevertheless, codes of conduct should also obviously be developed in those colleges and universities where teaching improprieties are well known and problematic. The development of a code of conduct communicates to the lay public the high value placed on undergraduate students as clients of teaching by the institution.

We advance a code of conduct for undergraduate college teaching to protect the interests of faculty, the institution, its various academic units, and undergraduate students. The development of institutional or departmental codes of conduct symbolizes an institutional readiness to engage in professional self-regulation of teaching improprieties. Accepting responsibility for professional self-regulation helps assure institutional and professorial autonomy in teaching. Institutional codes of conduct for undergraduate college teaching also serve undergraduate students by protecting their welfare, welfare centered on learning and personal development.

We urge individual colleges and universities, and their faculty, to adopt codes of conduct for undergraduate teaching. For many in the professoriate, the teaching role is far more salient than the research role. However, only the research role has associated normative standards reflected in codes of conduct and in existing institutional structures to address improprieties in the research enterprise. Our students, the clients of the professoriate, deserve equal protection to those that foster research integrity.

References

Boice, R. "Classroom Incivilities." *Research in Higher Education,* 1996, *37,* 453–485.

Braxton, J. M., and Bayer, A. E. *Faculty Misconduct in Collegiate Teaching.* Baltimore: Johns Hopkins University Press, 1999.

Decoo, W. *Crisis on Campus: Confronting Academic Misconduct.* Cambridge, Mass.: MIT Press, 2002.

Franke, A. H. "Faculty Misconduct, Discipline and Dismissal." Paper presented at the annual meeting of the National Association of College and University Attorneys, New Orleans, March 22, 2002.

Hamilton, N. W. *Academic Ethics: Problems and Materials on Professional Conduct and Shared Governance.* Washington, D.C.: American Council on Education and New York: Praeger, 2002.

Svinicki, M. "Ethics in College Teaching." In W. J. McKeachie (ed.), *Teaching Tips: Strategies, Research, and Theory for College and University Teachers.* (9th ed.) Lexington, Mass.: Heath, 1994.

Tabachnick, B. G., Keith-Speigel, P., and Pope, K. S. "Ethics of Teaching: Beliefs and Behaviors of Psychologists as Educators." *American Psychologist,* 1991, *46,* 506–515.

JOHN M. BRAXTON *is professor of education in the Higher Education Leadership and Policy Program, Peabody College, Vanderbilt University.*

ALAN E. BAYER *is professor of sociology, adjunct professor of science studies, and director of the Center for Survey Research at Virginia Polytechnic Institute and State University.*

PART THREE

Student Rights and Improprieties

7

Student perceptions of what constitutes appropriate and inappropriate classroom behavior are affected by who is being asked.

Student Norms of Classroom Decorum

Timothy C. Caboni, Amy S. Hirschy, Jane R. Best

The improvement of undergraduate instruction has received considerable attention in recent years. Many recommendations for improvement have been made, including how to enhance the teaching and learning process (Braxton, Olsen, and Simmons, 1998). However, one area of classroom behavior that has not received a great deal of inquiry is that of classroom disturbances and misbehavior, frequently referred to as classroom incivilities. Experts on college teaching have resisted empirical evaluations of classroom incivility (Weimer and Lenze, 1991). In addition, the higher education literature pays scant attention to these behaviors (Boice, 1996). When they are studied, researchers tend to examine classroom incivilities abstractly or in an indirect way (Boice, 1996). The problem has been discussed as a mental health problem (Amada, 1992), as an issue of student course preference (Wyatt, 1992), as an issue of student perceptions of a class's value in a future career (Didner, 1992), and as an issue of personality conflict between teachers and students (Appleby, 1990).

Pascarella and Terenzini (1991) conclude from their extensive review of literature on the effects of college on students that peers exert considerable influence on the cognitive and affective development of college students. Student peers also influence the behavior of their peer group members (Newcomb, 1966; Kuh and Whitt, 1988). Despite the importance of peers in the classroom environment, little research has focused on the empirical delineation of what college students perceive as inappropriate classroom behaviors. To date, there has been no empirical evaluation of the role of social control in the occurrence of classroom incivilities. The study reported here posits that if we understand which classroom behaviors students perceive as inappropriate, we may begin to understand the type of

NEW DIRECTIONS FOR TEACHING AND LEARNING, no. 99, Fall 2004   © Wiley Periodicals, Inc.

influence student peers have on the behavior of other students within the classroom, specifically as it relates to classroom incivilities.

Thus, the purpose of this chapter is to present the findings of an exploratory study designed to identify those in-class behaviors perceived as inappropriate by students at one university. This research also focuses on the influence of student characteristics—gender, race or ethnicity, class standing, and social fraternity or sorority membership—on these behaviors.

Conceptual Framework

The number of uncivil behaviors that occur in university classrooms is increasing (Sorcinelli, 1994; Amada, 1994). Although the frequency of such disruptions is growing, the topic is largely absent from the higher education literature. Boice (1996) suggests that classroom incivilities may not receive appropriate attention from higher education researchers for four reasons: discussion of classroom incivilities are taboo and embarrassing; accounts of student incivility are more prevalent among teachers with lower status; other doctoral-level practitioners, such as therapists, acknowledge incivility more readily; and higher education researchers tend to approach the subject of classroom incivility abstractly and indirectly.

Hersch (1998) argues that adolescents' lives are isolated from the lives of adults, and that along with peers, adolescents create their own rules, regulations, rituals, and behavioral expectations. College students use the rules devised by their peers, which may be different from those expected by adults. As a result, the adult world perceives many of the rules associated with these subgroups as disruptive (Hernandez and Fister, 2001).

In addition to language, values, practices, and beliefs, norms are a central characteristic of peer groups (Kuh and Whitt, 1988). Norms are prescriptive and proscriptive patterns of behavior (Hechter and Opp, 2001; Merton, 1968, 1973). These patterns delineate behavior expected in certain situations or circumstances that are shared by members of a particular social group (Gibbs, 1981; Rossi and Berk, 1985). They also regulate the social behavior of group members (Hechter and Opp, 2001; Horne, 2001).

The index of a norm's social significance rests in the degree of moral outrage or indignation such proscribed behaviors elicit (Durkheim, 1995). Moral outrage can be assessed by determining the severity of sanctions students perceive as warranted by proscribed behaviors. Conversely, the social significance of prescribed or appropriate behaviors is manifested in the degree of strong approval such prescribed behaviors invoke. Strong approval can be ascertained by identifying the type of rewards student perceive to be justified by prescribed behaviors.

Previous research on the influence of norms on the behaviors of various groups on college and university campuses demonstrates the utility of norms as a window into the behavior of college and university subgroups. Braxton and Bayer (1999) found normative patterns used by the academic profession for self-regulation. Caboni (2003) describes similar patterns for fundraising professionals on college and university campuses. In addition, normative support has been found for Chickering and Gamson's principles (1987) of good undergraduate education for both faculty (Braxton, Eimers, and Bayer, 1996) and students (Caboni, Mundy, and Duesterhaus, 2003). These formulations provide the framework for the empirical identification of a normative structure that may restrain students from engaging in classroom incivilities.

Student characteristics form sources of personal control. Personal controls are characterized as the individual's ability to avoid norm violations that may occur as a result of personal needs (Reiss, 1951). Obversely, personal controls reflect the individual's ability to engage in strongly approved behaviors because of personal needs. By extension, personal controls may also influence the student espousal of proscribed and prescribed normative orientations. Thus, such student characteristics as gender, race or ethnicity, class standing, and membership in a social fraternity or sorority may influence student espousal of both the prescribed and proscribed normative orientations identified in this research. Such student characteristics are posited to be personal sources of control because research has demonstrated their influence on college students' cognitive and affective development (Pascarella and Terenzini, 1991).

Research Questions

This study focuses on the norms espoused by students and whether these norms might be used by student peer groups within the classroom to regulate uncivil behaviors. First, we identified the behaviors associated with classroom incivilities. In relation to these behaviors, we asked the following two research questions:

1. *Is there normative support for sanctioning classroom incivilities at this institution?* By examining the classroom behaviors students at this institution perceive as inappropriate, we may more fully understand the level of student sanctioning in place that may restrict these behaviors.

2. *If student norms do exist that regulate inappropriate classroom behaviors, how do these differ between different groups of students?* Specifically we ask, Are there significant differences between different groups of students in their perceptions of the level of inappropriateness ascribed to each of these normative patterns?

Method

The subjects for this study were randomly selected from the undergraduate population of a predominately residential, Research-I university with admissions selectivity ranked as most competitive. Individuals were randomly selected from the database of students living in residence halls. One thousand students were selected to receive a copy of the questionnaire during spring 2000. Of those, 214 (21.4 percent) returned completed surveys. The low response rate may be due in part to the inability of the researchers to employ multiple mailing waves. The results are from a single distribution of the instrument. Individuals who returned questionnaires could not be identified and could not be recontacted to increase the response rate.

The respondents were closely matched to the overall undergraduate profile except in the case of men, fraternity members, and sorority members, who were underrepresented (greater or less than a 5 percent difference between the sample and population).

To measure the degree to which these students felt that various behaviors could be considered norms of classroom behavior, two composite variables were created and evaluated as measures of broad categories of classroom incivility outlined by Boice (1996). The sets of statements used in relation to both of the classroom incivilities appear in Table A.2 in the Appendix. These two variables are *disrespectful disruption* and *insolent inattention*. Disrespectful disruption refers to an active behavior in which a student engages that impedes learning by other members of a class. Repetitive disruption of others, receiving cellular telephone calls, or departing class before the professor excuses the group are all examples of disrespectful disruption. The pattern of insolent inattention describes student behaviors that demonstrate an inability or unwillingness to pay attention to classroom activities. A student who attends class intoxicated and is unable to participate due to his or her physical condition would be engaging in insolent inattention. While both of these types of behaviors may disturb the classroom environment, the primary difference is the degree to which a student engages in these behaviors in an active or passive manner. Students responded on a scale of one to nine, with one indicating a very inappropriate behavior and nine indicating a very appropriate behavior.

We classified these clusters of behaviors as a norm only if in the aggregate they elicited a strong response from the students (mean of less than 3.5). This level suggests that students believe that engaging in these behaviors requires the application of a sanction. A value of 3.0 represents "inappropriate behavior, someone should talk to the student about the behavior and suggest change or improvement." A value of 4.0 represents "mildly inappropriate behavior, generally to be ignored." The 3.5 level represents the point at which a behavior could no longer be ignored. This follows the approach of Caboni, Mundy, and Duesterhaus (2003) and Braxton, Eimers, and Bayer (1996) to determine normative support of students and faculty for undergraduate teaching recommendations.

What Do Students Consider a "Norm"?

The results of this study reveal several important findings related to incivilities in university classrooms. In regard to the first question posed by the research, "Is there normative support for sanctioning classroom incivilities

Table 7.1. Means and Standard Deviations for the Two Normative Patterns Regulating Classroom Incivilities

Normative Pattern	Mean*	Standard Deviation
Disrespectful disruption	3.71	0.52
Insolent inattention	2.67	0.51

Note: *Scale 1–9; 1 = very inappropriate.

Table 7.2. Effects of Gender

Normative Pattern	Mean Male	Mean Female	t-value
Disrespectful disruption	3.73	3.71	0.28
Insolent inattention	2.80	2.45	2.75**

Note: ** $p < .01$

Table 7.3. Effects of Group Membership

Normative Pattern	F-Ratio	Fraternities Means	Sororities Means	Non-affiliated Means
Disrespectful disruption	5.00**	4.08	3.68	3.68
Insolent inattention	9.03**	3.28	2.34	2.57

Note: ** $p < .01$

at this institution?" we found normative support for one pattern in the aggregate that prohibits classroom incivility. The broad category of classroom incivility proscribed is insolent inattention. We did not find normative support for the construct disrespectful disruption. Table 7.1 displays the statistical information used to make these observations.

Our second question asked, "Are there significant differences between different groups of students in their perceptions of the level of inappropriateness ascribed to the normative patterns?" Both gender and Greek organization membership affected the espousal of the inappropriate nature of the normative pattern insolent inattention. In general, males perceived insolent inattention as less inappropriate than females. In addition, members of social fraternities perceived the normative pattern as less inappropriate than did members of social sororities and non-affiliated students. Regarding the pattern disrespectful disruption, fraternity members perceived this set of behaviors as significantly less inappropriate than either sorority members or non-affiliated students. However, it should be noted that none of the subgroups of students regarded disrespectful disruption as a normative pattern. Tables 7.2 and 7.3 provide supporting results of statistical analyses.

Implications of These Results

The study has several implications for college teachers and institutional policymakers. These include policy levers available to administrators to manage classroom incivilities, issues of normative incongruence between faculty and students, and issues surrounding Greek life on campuses.

Campus Policies Regarding Classroom Incivilities. Amada (1994) suggests that institutional policies may be developed to address the disruptive behavior of students. Without an understanding of what students (or subgroups of students) on a campus perceive as inappropriate classroom behaviors, institutional policies may not be as effective as they might if student norms of classroom incivility are taken into account in policy formation. Durkheim (1995) suggests that norms reflect the "collective conscience" of a social group. In other words, norms index deep-seated values of a particular social group (Braxton and Bayer, 1999). Because norms tap into entrenched values, policies implemented by administrators may not prove effective at reducing or eliminating intended behaviors. If norms do not buttress administrative policies, when sanctions are applied there may be a temporary suspension of the behavior in question. However, because informal norms are not in place to discourage the behavior, there is an increased likelihood the violation will recur.

Normative Incongruence. As Boice (1996) notes, classroom incivilities are caused by both students and faculty. This study suggests that students play an important role in sanctioning the behaviors of their class peers. However, if a faculty member perceives a set of behaviors as being inappropriate but students do not, this may become problematic for both parties. For example, if members of a social fraternity do not perceive disrespectful disruption as reaching normative criteria but faculty do find behaviors associated with this pattern as inappropriate, the disjuncture between these two groups (or individual members of each of these groups) may cause friction within the classroom. This normative incongruence may place additional strain on the faculty member attempting to eliminate classroom incivilities, because normative support may not exist within the student's peer group. This incongruence may also operate at a more general level, with individual students who do not perceive behaviors as being as inappropriate as campus peers being more likely to feel uncomfortable. These individuals may feel as if they do not fit in with the rest of the student body. Durkheim (1951) suggests that individuals are integrated because they possess similar beliefs and values as the community. They also share or possess similar norms. Conversely, if students are in a state of normative incongruence, they may be more likely to depart the institution. This may be another lens through which we may view college persistence and departure.

Greek Life. As administrators on college campuses evaluate their Greek systems, this study adds to previous studies that examine the influence of fraternities on their members. Caboni, Mundy, and Duesterhaus (2003) found that members of social fraternities provided less normative support to the implementation of good practices in undergraduate teaching. Moreover, members of social fraternities may perceive more broadly defined inappropriate behaviors as significantly less inappropriate than their college peers (Caboni, Braxton, and Mundy, forthcoming).

Concluding Thoughts

The findings from this study suggest that patterns exist that proscribe inappropriate classroom behaviors. In addition, the findings suggest that these normative patterns are influenced by gender and Greek organization membership. More fully understanding how social forces influence classroom behaviors may lead to more intentionality in crafting campus policies and interventions, and to increased faculty awareness of challenges in regulating student classroom behavior. This, in turn, may facilitate greater individual learning within college classrooms.

References

Amada, G. "Coping with the Disruptive College Student: A Practical Model." *Journal of American College Health*, 1992, *40*, 203–215.

Amada, G. *Coping with the Disruptive Student*. Asheville, N.C.: College Administration Publications, 1994.

Appleby, D. C. "Faculty and Student Perceptions of Irritating Behaviors in the College Classroom." *Journal of Staff, Program, and Organization Development*, 1990, *8*, 41–46.

Boice, R. "Classroom Incivilities." *Research in Higher Education*, 1996, *37*, 453–485.

Braxton, J. M., and Bayer, A. E. *Faculty Misconduct in Collegiate Teaching*. Baltimore: Johns Hopkins University Press, 1999.

Braxton, J. M., Eimers, M. T., and Bayer, A. E. "The Implications of Teaching Norms for the Improvement of Undergraduate Education." *Journal of Higher Education*, 1996, *67*, 603–625.

Braxton, J. M., Olsen, D., and Simmons, A. "Affinity Disciplines and the Use of Principles of Good Practice for Undergraduate Education." *Research in Higher Education*, 1998, *39*, 299–318.

Caboni, T. C. "Toward Professionalism: Norms and Fund Raising." *The CASE International Journal of Educational Advancement*, 2003, *4*(1), 77–91.

Caboni, T. C., Braxton, J. M., and Mundy, M. E. "Toward an Empirical Delineation of a Normative Structure for College Students." *Journal of Higher Education*, forthcoming.

Caboni, T. C., Mundy, M. E., and Duesterhaus, M. B. "The Implications of the Norms of Undergraduate College Students for Faculty Enactment of Principles of Good Practice in Undergraduate Education." *Peabody Journal of Education*, 2003, *77*, 125–137.

Chickering, A. W., and Gamson, Z. E. "Seven Principles for Good Practice in Undergraduate Education." *AAHE Bulletin*, 1987, *39*, 3–7.

Didner, J. "Survey Reveals High Level of Academic Fraud." *Stony Brook Statesman*, February 10, 1992, pp. 1–2.

Durkheim, E. *Suicide*. (J. A. Spaulding and G. Simpson, trans.). New York: Free Press, 1951.

Durkheim, E. *The Elementary Forms of Religious Life*. New York: Free Press, 1995.

Gibbs, J. *Norms, Deviance and Social Control: Conceptual Matters.* New York: Elsevier, 1981.

Hechter, M., and Opp, K. (eds.). *Social Norms.* New York: Russell Sage Foundation, 2001.

Hernandez, T., and Fister, D. "Dealing with Disruptive and Emotional College Students: A Systems Model." *Journal of College Counseling,* 2001, *4*(1), 49–62.

Hersch, P. *A Tribe Apart: A Journey into the Heart of American Adolescence.* New York: Ballantine, 1998.

Horne, C. "Sociological Perspectives on the Emergence of Social Norms." In M. Hechter and K. Opp (eds.), *Social Norms.* New York: Russell Sage Foundation, 2001.

Kuh, G. D., and Whitt, E. J. *The Invisible Tapestry: Culture in American Colleges and Universities.* ASHE-ERIC Higher Education Report, no. 1. Washington, D.C.: American Association for Higher Education, 1988.

Merton, R. K. *Social Theory and Social Structure.* New York: Free Press, 1968.

Merton, R. K. *The Sociology of Science: Theoretical and Empirical Investigations.* Chicago: University of Chicago Press, 1973.

Newcomb, T., and Wilson, E. *College Peer Groups.* Chicago: Aldine, 1966.

Pascarella, E., and Terenzini, P. *How College Affects Students.* Jossey-Bass: San Francisco, 1991.

Reiss, A. J. "Delinquency as a Failure of Personal and Social Controls." *American Sociological Review,* 1951, *16*(2), 196–207.

Rossi, P., and Berk, R. "Varieties of Normative Consensus." *American Sociological Review,* 1985, *50*(3), 333–347.

Sorcinelli, M. D. "Dealing with Troublesome Behaviors in the Classroom." In K. W. Pritchard and R. M. Sawyer (eds.), *Handbook of College Teaching: Theory and Applications.* Westport, Conn.: Greenwood Press, 1994.

Weimer, M., and Lenze, L. F. "Instructional Interventions: A Review of the Literature on Efforts to Improve Instruction." In J. C. Smart (ed.), *Higher Education: Handbook of Theory and Research.* New York: Agathon, 1991.

Wyatt, G. "Skipping Class: An Analysis of Absenteeism Among First Year Students." *Teaching Students,* 1992, *20,* 201–207.

TIMOTHY C. CABONI is a lecturer in public policy and higher education and director of the institutional advancement specialization in the Higher Education Leadership and Policy Program, Peabody College, Vanderbilt University.

AMY S. HIRSCHY is assistant professor in the Department of Educational and Counseling Psychology and the Department of Leadership, Foundations, and Human Resource Education at the University of Louisville.

JANE R. BEST has a Ph.D. in higher education leadership and policy studies from Vanderbilt University.

Student violations of behavior norms affect the learning of others, the teaching of the instructor, and the atmosphere of the classroom.

8

Effects of Student Classroom Incivilities on Students

Amy S. Hirschy, John M. Braxton

Based on extensive academic and political attention to the need for improving the undergraduate learning experience, strong interest exists in understanding how students succeed in college and what factors impede their progress (Boyer, 1987; Chickering and Gamson, 1987; Ewell and Jones, 1996; Study Group on the Conditions of Excellence in American Higher Education, 1984). A rich vein of the literature focuses on the effects of classroom interactions between faculty and students and among students as peers (Feldman and Paulsen, 1998; Pascarella and Terenzini, 1991). With the goals of improving undergraduate education and understanding faculty roles, scholars have expanded the view of scholarship to include teaching (Boyer, 1990), recommended changes to the faculty evaluation process on the role of teaching (Glassick, Huber, and Maeroff, 1997), specified teaching role performance norms in the classroom (Braxton and Bayer, 1999), and identified classroom incivilities (Appleby, 1990; Boice, 1996a).

Scholars address aspects of the nature and frequency of classroom incivilities displayed by instructors and students. They also consider how faculty can reduce and deal with classroom incivilities (Amada, 1999; Appleby, 1990; Boice, 1996a; Feldmann, 2001; Kearney and Plax, 1992; Sorcinelli, 1994).

Both faculty and students consider certain behaviors irritating in the classroom. Appleby (1990) identifies faculty and student perceptions that negatively affect the teaching and learning process. Faculty report being most irritated by immature and inattentive students, and students reveal being most annoyed with teachers who are unempathetic and poor communicators. Boice (1996b) found that students and faculty agree on ranking three kinds of classroom incivilities as strongly disturbing: students conversing so loudly that lecturers and student discussants could not be heard throughout a third or more of class meetings, students confronting teachers with sarcastic remarks, and the presence of one or two "classroom terrorists" whose unpredictable and highly emotional outbursts (such as insulting or intimidating disagreements) made the class tense (p. 11).

Boice discusses the effects of student classroom incivilities on faculty, student classroom behavior, and student course ratings (1996a) and offers advice to faculty on how to mediate and address behaviors that influence the learning process negatively (1996b, 2000). However, research to understand the effects of disruptive classroom behavior on students beyond the classroom remains underdeveloped. Classroom incivilities may affect the academic and intellectual development of students negatively and reduce their commitment to their college or university, both of which can impede a student's progress toward his or her educational goals. This chapter focuses on the effects of classroom incivilities by students on other students. The purpose of this chapter is to describe the findings of a study that focuses on the effects of student classroom incivilities on student academic and intellectual development and on their commitment to their college or university.

Classroom Incivilities

Classroom incivilities are actions that hinder a "harmonious and cooperative learning atmosphere in the classroom" (Feldmann, 2001, p. 137). Examples of student classroom incivilities include arriving late to class and leaving early in a disruptive manner. Hernandez and Fister (2001) characterize disruptive student classroom behaviors as rebellious, emotional, or escalating in nature. Rebellious behaviors tend to be intentional and disrespectful. Students who continue to talk with others after they have been asked not to display rebellious disruptive behaviors. In contrast to rebellious behaviors, emotionally disruptive behaviors appear to be unintentional. Students who are unable to control their emotional distress may exhibit disruptive behaviors, including unintended outbursts, excessive absences, or leaving the classroom unexpectedly. Some students show escalating disruptive classroom behaviors by exhibiting both rebellious and emotional behaviors. Students who need excessive attention in the classroom and whose behavior leads to aggressive acts demonstrate escalating behaviors.

According to Boice (1996a), incidents of classroom incivilities are "more common than uncommon" (p. 479), and occur regardless of the level of teaching experience of the instructor. Effective teachers tend to be more skillful in using positive motivators (such as asking students if they understand, encouraging students that they can do better), and expressing immediacies (such as making eye contact with students, showing students that they care). Patterns of classroom incivilities are often established within the first four days of classes, though pivotal events during the semester can shift the number of classroom incivilities in a course.

Both instructors and students play an active role in defining the interactions among classroom participants. Faculty members structure the learning environment in a classroom in several ways. A teacher's preparation, pedagogical approach, or intervention may foster a classroom environment that supports respectful discourse among classmates and advances other effective learning conditions for students. Fassinger (1995) found that student traits, such as confidence levels, and class traits, such as supportive classmates, were better predictors of student participation than instructor traits, such as approachability and discussion style. This suggests that instructors can have the greatest impact on classroom interactions through designing their courses to include forms of cooperative and collaborative learning. Through these methods, faculty members can reduce student classroom incivilities, but students clearly play an important role in shaping the classroom climate.

Peer Effects on Academic and Intellectual Development

Research findings on classroom interaction and its effect on learning affirm that student peers have a significant influence on the norms of the classroom by how the class members interact. Peers can effectively hinder or encourage their classmates' involvement (Colbeck, Campbell, and Bjorklund, 2000; Fassinger, 1997; Hallinan and Smith, 1989). Further, a supportive classroom environment is related to higher levels of participation (Fassinger, 1997; Reynolds and Nunn, 1997), and a student's level of participation is positively correlated to intellectual skill development (Terenzini, Theophilides, and Lorang, 1984a). In their extensive compilation of research on college students, Pascarella and Terenzini (1991) cite research that offers substantial evidence that peer classroom interactions have direct, positive effects on student academic and personal development (for example, Pike, 1989; Strauss and Volkwein, 2002; Terenzini, Pascarella, and Lorang, 1982; Terenzini, Springer, Pascarella, and Nora, 1995; Terenzini, Theophilides, and Lorang, 1984a and 1984b; Volkwein and Carbone, 1994), as well as empirical support for the powerful nature of peer influence on college students beyond the classroom (for example, Astin, 1984; Kuh, Schuh, Whitt, and Associates, 1991).

Student Commitment to the Institution

Tinto's interactionalist theory of college student departure primarily addresses voluntary student departure decisions within institutions, gleaning its theoretical grounding from Durkheim's sociological theory of suicide (1951) and that of Spady (1970), who first connected Durkheim's ideas to the study of college student persistence (Tinto, 1993). An attempt to account for the informal and formal influences the institution has on the decision for students to leave, Tinto's model is comprised of fifteen logically related propositions that lead to student departure or persistence. By reviewing empirical studies on student persistence, Braxton, Sullivan, and Johnson (1997) assessed Tinto's theory, using thirteen testable propositions, including the link between a student's subsequent commitment to the institution and the student's decision to reenroll at the same institution. Through their review, the researchers found strong support for the influence of subsequent institutional commitment on student persistence. Therefore, identifying influences on a student's subsequent institutional commitment makes an important contribution to the literature on student persistence.

Institutional Type

According to the 1994 edition of the Carnegie Classification, comprehensive (CUC-II) colleges and universities typically award a full range of baccalaureate programs, plus twenty or more master's degrees. Baccalaureate-I (BA-I) institutions are primarily undergraduate colleges with a major emphasis on baccalaureate programs. Their admissions policies are selective and at least 40 percent of the degrees they grant are in the liberal arts field. Baccalaureate-II (BA-II) colleges are similar to BA-I institutions, except that less than 40 percent of the degrees they grant are in the liberal arts field and their admissions policies are less selective (Hirschy, 2003).* According to Tom (1998), the norms of classroom incivilities will likely vary by type of institution.

Critical Questions

This chapter focuses on the following three questions:

1. What are the effects of student classroom incivilities on student academic and intellectual development?
2. What are the effects of student classroom incivilities on student commitment to their college or university?
3. Does institutional type make a difference in the effects of student classroom incivilities?

The details of the methodology underlying this chapter's study are found in the Appendix of this volume.

There are two variables of interest for this study. The first is student perceptions of their academic and intellectual development. This variable is measured as a composite of five survey items included on the *National Assessment of College Student Classroom Experience Survey*. The second dependent variable is subsequent institutional commitment (see Table A.3 in the Appendix for measurements of both variables). Two forms of student classroom incivilities were included as independent variables in this inquiry, disrespectful disruption and insolent inattention as described in Chapter Seven (see Table A.2 in the Appendix for their measurement). In addition to the two classroom incivilities variables, we included five control variables in this research design: gender, class standing, cumulative grade-point average, informal faculty and student interactions, and academic major (in high- and low-consensus disciplines). These five variables represent possible rival hypotheses to the influence of the two forms of student classroom incivilities on the academic and intellectual development of students. Thus, we control for these variables in this study (see Table A.3 in the Appendix for their measurement). We also control for class standing, as juniors and seniors will likely perceive greater levels of academic and intellectual development than will first-year students and sophomores. Students with higher cumulative grade-point averages are also more likely to perceive greater levels of academic and intellectual development.

Do Incivilities Affect Achievement and Persistence?

The two classroom incivilities, disrespectful disruption and insolent inattention, are indeed able to explain a statistically significant portion of the variance in both achievement and persistence. Findings indicate that both forms of student classroom incivilities affect student perceptions of their own academic and intellectual development negatively. Both forms of incivilities also influence student commitment to their college or university in a negative way. This configuration of findings is above and beyond the effects of class standing, gender, faculty-student interactions, and grade-point average. Table A.6 in the Appendix supports these assertions.

The findings of this study affirm the need for instructors and those who prepare faculty for their teaching roles to address classroom incivilities, as the disruptions to the classroom climate can lead to serious consequences for student success. In addition, further inquiry into the difference in students' perceptions of classroom incivilities at various institutional types would help institutions tailor their policies to the problems most likely to arise in their settings.

Instructors are hesitant to confront classroom incivilities (Sorcinelli, 1994). Acknowledging classroom incivilities is embarrassing, even taboo (Boice, 1996a). Fear of the consequences of disciplining a student may also influence a faculty member to remain silent about disruptive behaviors in the classroom (Amada, 1999). Moreover, faculty members may be reluctant to share details with their colleagues about disruptive behaviors and how they reacted to the students. Such reticence can lead faculty to feel isolated, frustrated, and incompetent (Hernandez and Fister, 2001). Feldmann (2001) offers two basic reasons for recognizing and addressing incivilities. First, failure to confront uncivil acts damages the learning environment. Second, challenging classroom incivilities can avert future disruptive behaviors from the same and other students.

This study indicates that the consequences of ignoring classroom incivilities can have deleterious effects on students, as the findings support that classroom incivilities harm the classroom climate. Further, the effects of classroom incivilities extend beyond the confines of the classroom and can damage students' efforts to succeed at their institutions. High incidents of disrespectful disruption and insolent inattention in the classroom affect student perceptions of their own academic and intellectual development negatively. Students who frequently observe classroom incivilities may spend less energy thinking critically during the class and be less engaged with the course material afterward. It follows that being distracted from class discussions and the concomitant connections to learning more deeply may affect students' satisfaction of their academic and intellectual development. Classroom incivilities can also undermine reciprocity and cooperative learning among students and adversely affect contact between students and faculty, two of the seven principles for good practice in undergraduate education developed by Chickering and Gamson (1987).

Both forms of incivilities in this study also significantly influence a student's commitment to his or her institution in a negative way. Students who become frustrated with a chaotic classroom environment due to student classroom incivilities may feel isolated and sense that their values, beliefs, and attitudes do not fit with those of other students. Isolation and normative incongruence are the central components of Durkheim's conception of integration (1951). Tinto's theory of student departure (1993) postulates that students who are insufficiently integrated into the social and academic realms of the institution will experience a decline in their commitment to their college or university. Previous research indicates that subsequent institutional commitment is empirically linked to persistence (Braxton, Sullivan, and Johnson, 1997). Put differently, curbing student classroom incivilities can have a positive, direct effect on subsequent commitment to the institution and a positive, indirect effect on student retention.

Results of the analyses in this study also show that there is a difference among the three institutional types on both disrespectful disruption and insolent inattention. Students in baccalaureate colleges-II and comprehensive colleges and universities-II perceived a significantly higher number of classroom incivilities compared to students in baccalaureate colleges-I. Possible explanations for the difference could be related to institutional selectivity or class size. Students enrolled in the more selective baccalaureate colleges-I may be more committed to their academic endeavors and to their institution. Regarding class size, Boice's study (1996a) sampled large survey courses in lecture halls with student enrollments of more than one hundred, more typical of larger institutions. The nature and number of incivilities in classrooms with smaller enrollments may differ from his sample. More research is necessary to understand the differences found in types of institution.

Implications for Policy and Practice

Although abundant efforts have been directed at improving nonacademic areas of institutions, work remains in responding to the research to adjust the academic experiences of students (Tinto, 1998). Phrased differently, a gap exists between research and practice with regard to the teaching and learning process. The findings of this study can have a swift impact on institutional policy and practice, as classroom incivilities often serve as effective predictors of how semesters and teaching careers unfold (Boice, 2000). Thus, faculty and administrators share an investment in understanding and reducing classroom incivilities.

Faculty members can prevent some classroom incivilities by reflecting on their teaching methods and making both proactive and reactive adjustments to how they manage the classroom (Boice, 1996b; Feldmann, 2001). Also, by showing students they genuinely care about them, instructors help foster respect in the classroom (Kilmer, 1998; McKeachie, 2002). Sorcinelli (1994) offers four strategies that instructors can use to create a positive classroom environment: define expectations for student behavior in the class, reduce student anonymity, seek feedback from students, and encourage active learning. In addition, the author provides specific suggestions of ways teachers can constructively address a variety of classroom incivilities, such as inattention, unpreparedness, and lateness.

Disruptive classroom behaviors can be addressed informally, through disciplinary action, and through consultation with other college and university officials, such as counseling professionals. Hernandez and Fister (2001) recommend a comprehensive, systemic approach to address disruptive behaviors in the college community effectively, including classroom incivilities. They offer institutional leaders several suggestions regarding methods to deal with disruptive students, all of which are applicable to addressing classroom incivilities. First, college and university officials can provide a faculty liaison who is familiar with the policies and procedures of the institution and with whom faculty members can talk about difficult students. Second, a faculty and staff handbook should include written descriptions of the related policies and procedures on faculty, staff, and student rights and responsibilities. Third, on-going training should be available to assist instructors and staff in identifying and addressing disruptive behavior when (or shortly after) it occurs.

Acknowledging that disruptive behaviors occur in the classroom and offering techniques to manage difficult situations may help faculty members feel less isolated and more prepared to deal with classroom improprieties. Recognizing the immense influence of incivilities on student and faculty experiences in the classroom and beyond may inspire institutional leaders to better prepare and support graduate students, new faculty, and experienced faculty for teaching. Teaching and learning centers, professional development initiatives, graduate faculty preparation programs, and faculty mentors could provide opportunities for instructors to hone their skills of reducing the negative effects of classroom incivilities.

Conclusion

The negative effects of student classroom incivilities occur within and extend beyond the classroom. Incidents of disrespectful disruption and insolent inattention hinder student academic and intellectual development and reduce student commitment to their college or university. Further, students in various types of institutions perceived classroom incivilities differently. Understanding the nature of classroom incivilities, strategies to prevent them, and techniques to address them can enhance both student and faculty success.

Note

*The Carnegie Classification system was revised in 2000. See http://www. carnegiefoundation.org for descriptions of the new categories.

References

Amada, G. *Coping with Misconduct in the College Classroom.* Asheville, N.C.: College Administration Publications, 1999.

Appleby, D. C. "Faculty and Student Perceptions of Irritating Behaviors in the College Classroom." *Journal of Staff, Program, and Organizational Development,* 1990, *8,* 41–46.

Astin, A. W. "Student Involvement: A Developmental Theory for Higher Education." *Journal of College Student Personnel,* 1984, *25,* 297–308.

Boice, R. "Classroom Incivilities." *Research in Higher Education,* 1996a, *37,* 453–485.

Boice, R. *First-Order Principles for College Teachers. Ten Basic Ways to Improve the Teaching Process.* Bolton, Mass.: Anker, 1996b.

Boice, R. *Advice for New Faculty Members.* Needham Heights, Mass.: Allyn and Bacon, 2000.

Boyer, E. *College: The Undergraduate Experience.* New York: HarperCollins, 1987.

Boyer, E. L. *Scholarship Reconsidered: Priorities of the Professoriate.* New York: Carnegie Foundation for the Advancement of Teaching, 1990.

Braxton, J. M., and Bayer, A. E. *Faculty Misconduct in Collegiate Teaching.* Baltimore: Johns Hopkins University Press, 1999.

Braxton, J. M., Sullivan, A. S., and Johnson, R. "Appraising Tinto's Theory of College Student Departure." In J. Smart (ed.), *Higher Education: Handbook of Theory and Research* (Vol. XII). New York: Agathon, 1997.

Chickering, A. W., and Gamson, Z. F. "Seven Principles for Good Practice in Undergraduate Education." *AAHE Bulletin,* 1987, *39*(7), 3–7.

Colbeck, C. L., Campbell, S. E., and Bjorklund, S. A. "Grouping in the Dark: What College Students Learn from Group Projects." *Journal of Higher Education,* 2000, *71,* 60–83.

Durkheim, E. *Suicide.* (J. A. Spaulding and G. Simpson, trans.). New York: Free Press, 1951.

Ewell, P., and Jones, D. *Indicators of "Good Practice" in Undergraduate Education: A Handbook for Development and Implementation.* Boulder, Colo.: National Center for Higher Education Management Systems, 1996.

Fassinger, P. A. "Understanding Classroom Interaction: Students' and Professors' Contributions to Students' Silence." *Journal of Higher Education,* 1995, *66,* 82–96.

Fassinger, P. A. "Classes Are Groups." *College Teaching,* 1997, *45*(1), 22–26.

Feldman, K. A., and Paulsen, M. B. (eds.). *Teaching and Learning in the College Classroom.* New York: Simon & Schuster, 1998.

Feldmann, L. J. "Classroom Civility Is Another of Our Instructor Responsibilities." *College Teaching,* 2001, *49*(4), 137–140.

Glassick, C. E., Huber, M. T., and Maeroff, G. I. *Scholarship Assessed: Evaluation of the Professoriate.* San Francisco: Jossey-Bass, 1997.

Hallinan, M. T., and Smith, S. S. "Classroom Characteristics and Student Friendship Cliques." *Social Forces,* 1989, *67,* 898–919.

Hernandez, T. J., and Fister, D. L. "Dealing with Disruptive and Emotional College Students: A Systems Model." *Journal of College Counseling,* 2001, *4*(1), 49–62.

Hirschy, A. S. "Carnegie Classification." In J. W. Guthrie (ed.), *Encyclopedia of Education* (2nd ed., Vol. 1). New York: MacMillan Reference USA, 2003.

Kearney, P., and Plax, T. G. "Student Resistance to Control." In J. C. McCroskey (ed.), *Power in the Classroom.* Mahwah, N.J.: Erlbaum, 1992.

Kilmer, P. D. "When a Few Disruptive Students Challenge an Instructor's Plan: Constructive Questioning and Destructive Behavior." *Journalism and Mass Communication Educator,* 1998, *53,* 81–84.

Kuh, G. D., Schuh, J. H., Whitt, E. J., and Associates. *Involving Colleges: Successful Approaches to Fostering Student Learning and Development Outside the Classroom.* San Francisco: Jossey-Bass, 1991.

McKeachie, W. J. *McKeachie's Teaching Tips: Strategies, Research, and Theory for College and University Teachers.* Boston: Houghton Mifflin, 2002.

Pascarella, E. T., and Terenzini, P. T. *How College Affects Students.* San Francisco: Jossey-Bass, 1991.

Pike, G. R. "Background, College Experiences, and the ACT-COMP Exam: Using Construct Validity to Evaluate Assessment Instruments." *Review of Higher Education,* 1989, *13,* 91–117.

Reynolds, K. C., and Nunn, C. E. *Engaging Classrooms: Student Participation and Instructional Factors That Shape It.* Paper presented at the Association for the Study of Higher Education, Albuquerque, 1997.

Sorcinelli, M. D. "Dealing with Troublesome Behaviors in the Classroom." In R. M. Sawyer (ed.), *Handbook of College Teaching.* Westport, Conn.: Greenwood Press, 1994.

Spady, W. "Dropouts from Higher Education: An Interdisciplinary Review and Synthesis." *Interchange,* 1970, *1,* 64–85.

Strauss, L. C., and Volkwein, J. F. "Comparing Student Performance and Growth in 2- and 4-Year Institutions." *Research in Higher Education,* 2002, *43,* 133–161.

Study Group on the Conditions of Excellence in American Higher Education. *Involvement in Learning: Realizing the Potential of American Higher Education.* Washington, D.C.: National Institute of Education, 1984.

Terenzini, P. T., Pascarella, E. T., and Lorang, W. "An Assessment of the Academic and Social Influences on Freshman Year Educational Outcomes." *Review of Higher Education,* 1982, *5,* 86–110.

Terenzini, P. T., Springer, L., Pascarella, E. T., and Nora, A. "Influences Affecting the Development of Students' Critical Thinking Skills." *Research in Higher Education,* 1995, *36,* 23–29.

Terenzini, P. T., Theophilides, C., and Lorang, W. "Influences on Students' Perceptions of Their Academic Skill Development During College." *Journal of Higher Education,* 1984a, *55,* 621–636.

Terenzini, P. T., Theophilides, C., and Lorang, W. "Influences on Students' Perceptions of Their Personal Development During the First Three Years of College." *Review of Higher Education,* 1984b, *21,* 178–194.

Tinto, V. "Dropout from Higher Education: A Theoretical Synthesis of Recent Research." *Review of Educational Research*, 1975, *45*, 89–125.

Tinto, V. *Leaving College: Rethinking the Causes and Cures of Student Attrition.* (2nd ed.) Chicago: University of Chicago Press, 1993.

Tinto, V. "Colleges as Communities: Taking Research on Student Persistence Seriously." *Review of Higher Education*, 1998, *21*, 167–177.

Tom, G. "Faculty and Student Perceptions of Classroom Etiquette." *Journal of College Student Development*, 1998, *39*, 515–517.

Volkwein, J. F., and Carbone, D. A. "The Impact of Departmental Research and Teaching Climates on Undergraduate Growth and Satisfaction." *Journal of Higher Education*, 1994, *65*, 147–167.

AMY S. HIRSCHY is assistant professor in the Department of Educational and Counseling Psychology and the Department of Leadership, Foundations, and Human Resource Education at the University of Louisville.

JOHN M. BRAXTON is professor of education in the Higher Education Leadership and Policy Program, Peabody College, Vanderbilt University.

9

Students must learn to balance what they can expect from faculty with what they need to do themselves to make the classroom a safe and welcoming climate for everyone.

Promulgating Statements of Student Rights and Responsibilities

Alan E. Bayer

Throughout this volume, we have developed the theme that college and university students as well as their classroom instructors engage in classroom incivilities. These incivilities may not be frequent and severe; however, they are sufficiently pervasive to be of general concern to the academic community. Moreover, when they occur, they are detrimental to both the opportunities for learning by students and the optimal pedagogical performance by faculty (see Figure 1.1 in Chapter One). Unlike a number of other analyses addressing this behavior (such as Richardson, 1999), we expressly do *not* focus on the student as the exclusive locus of incivility.

Rather, following Boice (1996), we view classroom incivility as often emanating from the synergy between the incivilities of students and the incivilities of faculty members toward students. Indeed, Boice (1996) proposes that faculty-initiated classroom incivility and teaching improprieties are "more common than uncommon" (p. 479), and he claims that traditionally there is "too large a role [attributed] to students, too small a part to teachers" (p. 484). Dalton (1998) advances this observation by noting that teaching and learning are predicated on the "bedrock ethical integrity of teachers and students" (p. 11), and that when either faculty members or students violate the moral standard of academic integrity "they jeopardize the core integrity of the learning enterprise" (p. 11).

Even more explicitly, Benton (2004, p. C4) suggests that disrespectful behavior on the part of faculty, which subsequently alienates students, is even more pronounced than most would recognize. He says:

More often than not, when a student is disrespectful, it is because the student feels disrespected by the teacher. Even the most progressive teachers are disrespectful in a thousand subtle and not-so-subtle ways: facial expressions, body language, not remembering students' names, terse comments on papers, humiliating some students while playing favorites with others, making prejudicial judgments because a student looks like a model or an athlete. But, most of all, we do this by underestimating our students' intelligence and ability, by assuming that we not only know more about our subjects, but that we are superior to our students as human beings.

Given that the dynamic of classroom incivility is perhaps frequently a synergistic one involving inappropriate behavior on the part of students often combined with, or prompted by, misfeasance or malfeasance of the college teacher, we explore institutional policies and procedures that might be employed or extended to address more adequately both potential contributors to the problem. In Chapter Six we focused on faculty impropriety and possible institutional policy to address such circumstances. In this chapter, we focus on the student role regarding classroom incivilities.

In Chapter Five ("The Influence of Teaching Norm Violations on the Welfare of Students as Clients of College Teaching"), one recommendation was that institutions should address student rights and responsibilities more expressly. Some institutions already have relatively extensive documents pertaining to this; others have only rudimentary applicable policy statements. All could be strengthened. The locus of these statements is generally in a brief Student Code of Conduct, or in a Student Handbook, or similarly named document. A preceding chapter also noted that a student handbook would be enhanced if it also specified procedures that students may undertake in dealing with improprieties, particularly those perpetrated by instructors. While peer social control may sometimes be effective in dealing with another student's improprieties (see Chapter Seven, "Student Norms of Classroom Decorum"), the relative powerlessness of undergraduate students, together with their lack of understanding of the appropriate roles and behaviors of instructors, may make dealing with faculty members' improprieties more problematic.

Consequently, this chapter focuses on the student and three separate aids to addressing classroom incivility. First, we address the formalization of student rights, as they may be salient to the normative structure in academe. Second, we consider some of the key components of a student handbook that formalizes expectations regarding student behavior, together with the potential role of the faculty member's syllabus or other adjunctive class materials to address student incivility proactively. Third, we outline what procedural guidelines need to be incorporated into student handbooks or similar documents so that social control and reporting of incidents of improprieties can be enhanced.

Student Rights

Faculty committees on teaching, as well as academic administrators and student governance organizations, might advisedly promulgate statements of student rights and expectations. Various components of the teaching norms we have identified (Braxton and Bayer, 1999) could be recast in the form of rights and expectations that stipulate the type of classroom decorum and course content that students should reasonably expect from teaching faculty members. Students would be better able to detect faculty violations of teaching norms if they were familiar with the elements of such a statement of student rights regarding their opportunities for learning. Such statements would also encourage students as clients to report incidents of classroom improprieties to the department chair or other responsible administrator before the professorial misconduct has grown to a crisis level.

Below, we provide a number of illustrative, though not exhaustive, elements of a statement on students' rights to a positive environment for learning (which implies corresponding expectations for faculty). In this section, we draw in part on recommendations for college teaching practices as articulated in the popular, multiple-edition guidebook (McKeachie, 2002) first published in 1951 and periodically updated for the past half-century. Some of these student rights follow:

The right to instruction based on adequate preparation and planning by the teacher. Instructors who fail to plan and prepare for class sessions, or spend the class hour in an *ad hoc* fashion, are failing in their conscientious commitment to optimize the structured learning opportunity and experience for students.

The right to expect a faculty member to be interested in, and demonstrate commitment to, the role of teaching. Unfortunately, it is not unusual, particularly at research universities, for students to be informed on their first day of class that the instructor views her or his teaching as secondary and that her or his personal priority is research. Such disparaging remarks may lead the students to reduce their interest in the class or in higher education generally.

The right to have classes on the days and times stated in institutional schedules. Unless there are severe extenuating circumstances or cancellations of classes for sufficient reason scheduled and announced substantially in advance (usually on the syllabus), students should be able to expect that their classes will meet as advertised. In Cahn's discussion of teaching ethics (1994), he views failure of an instructor to meet one's class on time as an especially grievous act: "A simple but important principle is that teachers are obligated to begin all classes on time. I know of no more obvious sign of a lack of concern for one's students than coming to class late and thereby wasting the time of those who have arrived promptly" (p. 19).

The right to receive substantive course content and the opportunity to attain course objectives as specified by the published course description. Instructors who elect to deviate substantially or entirely from the college's or department's own description of course content and objectives violate the confidence that students should be able to put in the advertised curriculum.

The right to be given assignments and reading materials that facilitate the learning process in relation to course objectives. McKeachie (1994) notes that "[in] choosing reading materials the most important thing is that they fit. . . . [teaching]. . . . objectives. One of the most annoying and confusing practices to students is instructor disagreement with the textbook" (p. 13). An allied grievous practice is to designate required texts that are authored by the instructor but marginally related to the course or for which royalties are not forgone.

Entitlement to a just, fair, respectful, and non-authoritarian classroom environment. McKeachie (1986) states: "One of the barriers to student learning is that many professors see themselves as handing down learning from a celestial throne" (p. 250). Such an authoritarian demeanor, which is frequently linked to a lack of fairness and respect for students, creates an environment that violates students' basic right to learn.

Freedom to express one's opinion and to challenge those of the instructor. Openness and tolerance for a diversity of opinion, without fear of reprisal, is a central aspect of the educational process.

The right to confidentiality. Some scholars view the confidentiality inherent in college teacher-student relationships as parallel to that of doctor and patient or lawyer and client (Svinicki, 1994). Although federal and state laws prohibit many breaches of student confidentiality, these laws are too frequently ignored by faculty. Indeed, these laws are sometimes violated merely for instructor convenience (such as posting grades with individual identifiers or returning class papers in a manner where students can see comments or grades on other students' papers).

The right to know the system on which one is to be graded and to be fairly rewarded for one's course accomplishments or mastery of the course materials. A compelling principle of pedagogy is to convey to students the basis on which they will be evaluated and graded. This should be communicated early in the course, preferably in writing on the course syllabus. One of the grievous proscriptive norms identified by Braxton and Bayer (1999) is the concern of the professoriate for particularistic grading. Universalistic standards and grading criteria are bedrock inviolable norms that all students might readily and properly assume.

The right to access to the instructor outside of class time. Many, but by no means all, institutions of higher education prescribe that classroom instructors must hold office hours, often specifying the minimum number of hours per week that the instructors must be available to their students. Regardless of whether such a policy exists, undergraduate students should be able to rely on accessibility to instructional faculty—with posted office hours honored by the instructor and "do not disturb" signs generally absent from office doors.

The right of students to evaluate their course and teacher. There are many methods to evaluate teaching; McKeachie (1994) notes that "the ultimate criterion for evaluating teaching is student learning" (p. 313). Other methods include classroom visitation by other faculty, peer evaluation of syllabi, and committee review of student portfolios. But a key evaluation method involves the input of the clients: students. This is typically in the form of student rating forms on instruction—a tool that empowers students and provides them with the right to give feedback on their classroom experience. Such feedback presumably provides the instructor with cues for improvement and gives peer committees and administrators a means to assess instructional performance.

Student Responsibilities and Student Handbooks

There can be little presumption that all college students understand and internalize behavioral norms appropriate to their role as students within their academic setting. Perlmutter (2004) states: "Nothing about education is obvious to students. Most of us expect our students to have learned how to be students by the time they reach college. Yet many. . . . need help" (p. B15). Richardson (1999) suggests that "teachers. . . . use the classroom as a place [for students] to learn acceptable behavior" (p. 1), and the essays in his book largely focus on faculty response to classroom disruption, incivility, and cheating.

However, reactive response of faculty members to student classroom incivilities and misconduct may itself be disruptive to the classroom climate and learning environment. Proactive measures by instructors will generally yield articulation of student responsibilities that will have less deleterious long-term effects on the learning climate than would assertive response by the instructor to isolated uncivil events over multiple class sessions throughout the academic term.

As noted below, institutional policies that expressly address student incivilities within the confines of the classroom setting are generally scant. With the exception of a few small liberal arts and religiously affiliated institutions, these policies are generally viewed by members of the campus community as prerogatives of individual faculty members. The general abandonment of *in loco parentis,* together with the strong assertions of faculty autonomy at most U.S. institutions, even on matters concerning what most would consider uncivil or grossly improper student behavior, precludes blanket, institution-wide policies.

Consequently, specification of student responsibilities regarding the classroom and learning environment remains largely with the individual instructor. Thus, a significant proactive means to communicate student responsibilities is through the syllabus on the first day of class. Indeed,

McKeachie (1994) specifically suggests that the syllabus include "rules of classroom behavior" and advises, "in fact it is generally helpful to list the responsibilities of the student and those of the instructor" (p. 17). These rules will, of course, vary by instructor, but some more universal ones include statements regarding such uncivil student acts as ridiculing another student, interrupting someone who is speaking, and late, disruptive arrival to class.

Some instructors have gone beyond the syllabus and introduced a separate contract on classroom behavior to be signed by each student on the first day of class (Bartlett, 2004). One such example is shown in Figure 9.1. This contact, used by some faculty members in the marketing department at Western Illinois University, outlines expected student behavior and also obligates the instructor for similar courtesies, such as turning off one's cell phone and being on time to class. Student failure to abide by the contract influences the grades awarded by the instructor. Such a contract improved classroom civility and was generally positively received by students (Bartlett, 2004).

But these initiatives by individual faculty members do not mean that faculty autonomy precludes any institution-wide statements addressing student misconduct, and institutions should be able to promulgate such statements without faculty perceiving they are being preempted in their autonomy. Indeed, many institutions formalize prescriptive and proscriptive rules for students related to instruction and learning (as well as about student life in general) in codes of conduct or a student handbook.

In this section we present an overview of contents of selected codes of conduct or pertinent sections of student handbooks that address student responsibilities specifically related to the classroom or the context of learning (some of which may be adapted for inclusion in individual faculty member's syllabi). A convenience sample of fifteen large public and non-sectarian private institutions' Web sites were perused for copies of the texts of student codes of conduct or documents listed as student handbooks. Some of the characteristics and content of these sources are summarized below.

Perhaps most remarkable in a perusal of institutional publications on student conduct is the general lack of specification of improper conduct in the student-as-learner role. Most codes refer to prohibition of plagiarism and cheating; but most codes go little beyond these proscribed acts to other student behaviors relative to the learning environment, such as those related to classroom decorum.

In many cases, substantial discourse is devoted to definition and discussion of plagiarism and cheating. Some institutions provide extended examples of what is considered plagiarism, and some suggest remedies for these examples (most frequently emphasizing bibliographic attribution and use of quotation marks).

Cheating can be even more difficult to define. Few written codes provide sufficient clarity as to precisely what is entailed in what might be labeled as cheating. This is not surprising given the broad array of activities that might be defined as cheating. In one recent empirical research study, for example, Pincus and Schmelkin (2003) catalogue twenty-eight different "academically dishonest behaviors" and show that many are unclear or ambiguous, even to experienced college teachers. As Maramark and Maline (1993) note, this leaves "students confused about what specific activities constitute cheating or believing that less serious forms of cheating are acceptable" (p. 7).

Beyond addressing these two aspects of the classroom and the teaching-learning environment, codes and handbooks generally say little else in this regard. They generally do not even mention proper classroom decorum and courtesies, such as turning off cell phones, allowing others to speak, not entering the class late or leaving early in a disruptive manner, and so forth. Presumably, those standards of proscriptive and prescriptive student behaviors are delegated to the individual college teacher to transmit to students and to enforce. It is clear that there are an almost infinite variety of behaviors that might be addressed, and codes would be too cumbersome to attempt to delineate all. Yet codes might usefully be more comprehensive. The fact that not all possible situations can be covered can be acknowledged in the codes of conduct. That is, a statement of the following sort, which represents a composite summary of such statements derived from several institutions' documents, might be included: "Primary institutional regulations and policies are provided in this handbook to give students general notice of both expected and prohibited conduct. This information should be read broadly; it is not intended to define misconduct in all detail and in exhaustive terms."

This is not to say that codes of conduct or student handbooks do not often cover a breadth of other topics in addition to those expressly related to the classroom and learning process. It is frequently the case that these documents address such activities as hazing; residence hall behavior; possession of firearms and controlled substances; intimidation, harassment, and assault; vandalizing property; the creation and dissemination of computer viruses; and so forth. But matters related to proper behavior and civility in regard to the learning process and the classroom seldom extend beyond inclusion of information regarding plagiarism and academic cheating. With a caveat that information cannot be and is not exhaustive, institutions could foster classroom civility by extending discussion of both proper and disruptive student behaviors that are sanctioned by the institution.

Disciplinary and Procedural Guidelines

Most student handbooks provide adequate description of the institutional procedures employed in cases of student misconduct. Those institutions that do not provide such information should advisedly do so. There are several key components to the handbooks already usefully developed on many campuses.

Figure 9.1. Contract on Classroom Behavior

Most students exhibit appropriate behavior in class, but there is some disagreement on what "appropriate" behavior is. At times, a consumer culture creeps into the classroom, with students sometimes perceiving faculty as employees hired to serve them. This is not the appropriate comparison—a professor is not here to give you what you *want,* but rather to help you obtain what you *need.* A professor is more like a physician. Just as any doctor who tells you "everything is fine" so that you'll be happy (when everything isn't fine) should be sued for malpractice, any faculty member who gives you an "A" regardless of your performance or allows anything to happen primarily because that is what will make you happy is doing you and other students a disservice.

Learning is a group activity, and the behavior of each person in class in some way or the other affects the learning outcomes of others. If we keep these thoughts and the following rules in mind, the classroom experience will be a better one for everyone involved.

Rules:
1. Class begins promptly at the beginning of the class period. You should be in your seat and ready to start participating in class at that time. That same rule also applies to me—I should be ready at the start of class, which means having the technology operational.
   a. Always bring the required supplies and be ready to be actively engaged in the learning process. This communicates preparedness and interest.
   b. If you come into class after an assignment has already been passed back, please do *not* ask for your assignment until after the class is over. It's unfair to the other students in class to wait while the professor searches again for your paper because you weren't there the first time. Just ask for it after class, and I'll be happy to supply it to you.
   c. In deciding whether to attend class, please do not ask your professor if she/he is covering anything important on that day. The course is carefully planned out—every day is important.
2. If you bring a newspaper to class, put it away *before* the start of class. If you sat in a business meeting and read the *Wall Street Journal* while the boss was outlining a new strategy, you'd likely be fired or demoted. The same standard applies here. In return, I promise to listen when you are talking to me and to treat you with respect.
3. Similarly, do not study material from other classes during this class. If you feel that you must spend our class time studying or doing homework, please go to the library.
4. Turn your cell phone off or to vibrate before the start of class. I'll also turn mine off.
5. It is fine to bring a drink or a snack to class, as long as it isn't distracting. However, please remember that someone else will be coming into the room after your class is done, *so pick up your trash.* You wouldn't visit a friend's house and leave newspapers, cans, bottles, and wrappers lying around after you left, so please don't do it here.
6. I expect to have your attention for the full class period. This means:
   a. Avoid conversations with people sitting around you. It's a small room—even if you whisper, please realize that other people can certainly *see* you, and that's distracting to them (and to me.)
   b. *Do not* start zipping up your backpack and rustling papers before the end of the class period. There's sufficient time for you to get to your next class without disrupting the last few minutes of this class. If one person does it, it seems to trigger others to do it, and it makes the last few minutes (when announcements are often made) less than optimal for everyone.

Figure 9.1. (Continued) Contract on Classroom Behavior

7. If you know that you'll need to leave before the class is over, try to sit as close to the door as possible so as not to disrupt others. Similarly, if you arrive in class late, just slip in as quietly as possible and take the first available seat you come to.

8. If you are so tired that you cannot keep your head up, you should leave. I realize that environmental factors affect this, including warm rooms, dimmed lights, and material that may not be interesting to you. However, laying your head on the desk or sleeping in class is rude, and it is distracting to others. (Would you consider me rude if you invited me to a party and I slept on your sofa during the party?) I'll try to make class interesting, but remember that my primary goal is to teach you, not to entertain you.

9. Turn in assignments on time. Earthquake, fire, flood, and catastrophic illness are the only reasonable excuses for a late submission. You want the professor to know who you are for the right reasons.

10. Being courteous in class does not mean that you have to agree with everything that is being said. However, you will rarely get your way with anybody in life by being rude, overly aggressive, or just plain hostile. If you disagree with me (or I with you) it is a good idea to wait and discuss the situation when you are not angry.

11. The rules of the syllabus, content of the exams, content of lectures, and calculation of the grade you earned are not a starting point for negotiations. While I am always willing to work with students on an individual basis, I cannot negotiate individual terms with each student.

12. Your questions are not an imposition—they are welcome and one of the professional highlights of my day. Chances are, if you have a question, someone else is thinking the same thing but is too shy to ask it. Please ask questions! You'll learn more, it makes the class more interesting, and you are helping others learn as well. But when you have a question or comment, please raise your hand first. Blurting out a question or comment when someone else has already raised their hand is rude—it's like jumping ahead of someone else in line.

13. If emergencies arise that require an absence from a session, be sure to get the notes and all other information that was covered in class from a colleague you trust. Expecting the faculty member to outline the class session in an independent message to you is not realistic as a professor typically has approximately 100+ students in his/her classes each semester.

14. The time to be concerned about your grade is in the first fourteen weeks of the course, not in the last week.

_____   _____ / _____ / _____

_____
Student Name   Date
Professor

Source: Drea, J., and Associates, Western Illinois University. Cited in Bartlett, T., "Taking Control of the Classroom," _Chronicle of Higher Education,_ Sep. 17, 2004, pp. A8–A9. (http://chronicle.com/prm/weekly/documents/v51/i04/classroom.pdf)

A first component is a statement regarding student rights and due process. These parallel those of American citizens in everyday life. Included are rights to a fair hearing, presumption of innocence, the right to face accusers, the right to appeal, and the like.

A second component is related to the judicial process. This includes description of the panel that will adjudicate the complaint and the procedure for establishing the makeup of the panel, whether composed of all students, of faculty representatives, or some other method of constituting the panel. Procedures for appeal, and the person or body to which the appeal is made, are also included.

The third component is explication of the possible consequences resulting from the disciplinary process. This includes a description of the range of outcomes—from a finding of innocence and thus dismissal of the case, to mild reprimand and awarding of a failing grade in a course in question, to temporary suspension, to expulsion or revocation of the degree.

Comprehensive statement of these rights, procedures, and consequences may act as a deterrent to misconduct and incivilities. Thorough documentation of this information in a student handbook also serves to emphasize the importance that the institution attributes to maintaining a civil environment and a climate conducive to learning.

Summary and Conclusions

Although most experienced college and university teaching faculty members can share instances of improprieties and incivilities on the part of some of their students, we do not concur with sensationalistic accounts that depict the college classroom as spiraling into chaos and the new generations of students as introducing extreme new levels of disinterest and disruption to the learning process. Nonetheless, this chapter is devoted to amelioration of student improprieties and incivilities whenever they might occur through mechanisms readily available to campus faculty and administrators, and to the formulation of statements of principles and practice that can be developed in collaboration with students and student government organizations.

The procedures described in this chapter to address student improprieties include encouraging instructors to address student behaviors and expectations directly in the syllabus, or even in a separate classroom behavior contract executed with each student on the first day of class. In addition, most institutions might better focus on the development of a comprehensive code of conduct and a detailed student handbook. Colleges and universities are encouraged to review these documents, or in some cases prepare such documents, to assure a relatively comprehensive description of expected student conduct related to the learning environment. Discussion of conduct with regard to learning and the classroom might advisedly go beyond addressing only the issues of cheating and plagiarism.

Also recommended is inclusion of a detailed discussion of student rights. We propose two types of rights. The first are student rights concerning reasonable expectations they may have in regard to their classrooms and their instructors. The second are citizen rights that students retain within their institutional setting, particularly regarding hearings pertaining to academic dishonesty or incivility.

Moreover, a student handbook may expressly acknowledge and recognize the substantial power discrepancy between teacher and student (see Svinicki, 1994), while still encouraging students' actions in reporting significant faculty improprieties. Similarly, peer pressure might be acknowledged within the context of responsible peer social control of student misconduct.

Finally, the procedural guidelines and process for allegations of student misconduct should be extensively articulated. A description of procedures is present in documents available from most American colleges and universities, but an emphasis on these procedures, and possible consequences, may contribute to a more civil environment for learning.

References

Bartlett, T. "Taking Control of the Classroom." *Chronicle of Higher Education*, Sep. 17, 2004, pp. A8-A9.

Benton, T. H. "No Respect." *Chronicle of Higher Education*, Jan. 9, 2004, pp. C1, C4.

Boice, R. "Classroom Incivilities." *Research in Higher Education*, 1996, 37, 453–485.

Braxton, J. M., and Bayer, A. E. *Faculty Misconduct in Collegiate Teaching.* Baltimore: Johns Hopkins University Press, 1999.

Cahn, S. M. *Saints and Scamps: Ethics in Academia.* (Revised ed.) Lanham, Md.: Rowman and Littlefield, 1994.

Dalton, J. C. "Creating a Campus Climate for Academic Integrity." In D. D. Burnett, L. Rudolph, and K. O. Clifford (eds.), *Academic Integrity Matters.* National Association of Student Personnel Administrators Monograph Series, 1998, pp. 11–21. (ED 452 477)

Maramark, S., and Maline, M. B. *Academic Dishonesty Among College Students.* Washington, D.C.: U.S. Department of Education, 1993.

McKeachie, W. J. *Teaching Tips: A Guidebook for the Beginning College Teacher.* (8th ed.) Lexington, Mass.: Heath, 1986.

McKeachie, W. J. *Teaching Tips: Strategies, Research, and Theory for College and University Teachers.* (9th ed.) Lexington, Mass.: Heath, 1994.

McKeachie, W. J. *Teaching Tips: Strategies, Research, and Theory for College and University Teachers.* (11th ed.) Boston: Houghton Mifflin, 2002.

Perlmutter, D. D. "Thwarting Misbehavior in the Classroom." *Chronicle of Higher Education*, April 2, 2004, pp. B14-B15.

Pincus, H. S., and Schmelkin, L. P. "Faculty Perceptions of Academic Dishonesty." *Journal of Higher Education*, 2003, 74, 196–209.

Richardson, S. M. (ed.). *Promoting Civility: A Teaching Challenge.* New Directions for Teaching and Learning, no. 77. San Francisco: Jossey-Bass, 1999.

Svinicki, M. "Ethics in College Teaching." In W. J. McKeachie, *Teaching Tips: Strategies, Research, and Theory for College and University Teachers.* (9th ed.) Lexington, Mass.: Heath, 1994, pp. 269–277.

ALAN E. BAYER is professor of sociology, adjunct professor of science studies, and director of the Center for Survey Research at Virginia Polytechnic Institute and State University.

10

Based on the research reported in this volume, the authors offer recommendations for all affected parties.

Conclusions and Recommendations: Avenues for Addressing Teaching and Learning Improprieties

Alan E. Bayer, John M. Braxton

Misconduct and uncivil behavior by members of the American academic community are not new problems unique to the contemporary academy. However, even recently, the focus has largely been on faculty and student impropriety outside of the classroom and outside of the context of the formal teaching and learning environment. Regarding students, for example, institutional concentration has been on such activities as consumption of alcohol and use of drugs, and more recently on spectator incivility at collegiate sporting events. For faculty, emphasis has been on such grievous acts as falsification of academic credentials and misconduct in the domain of research and scholarship, particularly with regard to plagiarism, fabrication of data, and falsification of results.

In the teaching-learning domain, institutional focus on student improprieties has principally been concentrated on student cheating and plagiarism. For instructional faculty, the traditional values of academic freedom and autonomy have resulted in little attention to their transgressions, except in instances of moral turpitude and particularly regarding public disclosures of amorous relationships between faculty members and their students. In this volume, we expand this discourse on student and faculty incivilities and improprieties within the teaching-learning domain. This volume begins to catalog student incivilities in the classroom more broadly and identifies the range of incidents of faculty misconduct in relation to collegiate teaching. We also explore the impacts that these deviant acts—both by peers and by the professoriate—may have on student learning. Moreover, following Boice

(1996), we note the potential synergistic interplay between incivilities of faculty toward students and the uncivil behavior of students that sometimes results.

In this chapter, we summarize an array of institutional policies and procedures that might be employed or extended to address both potential contributors, students and faculty members, to the problem of incivilities related to the teaching and learning environment in college classrooms and on American college campuses. Clearly, these are not intended to be exhaustive. Similarly, this chapter catalogues some next steps for research on campus incivility, including the interplay between incivilities by students and misfeasance and malfeasance by instructional faculty members. These too are illustrative of some core focal points needed in future research and are obviously not intended to be an exhaustive discussion of needed research avenues.

Policies and Procedures Addressing Incivilities

In this section, we summarize some of the possible institutional responses that have been proposed in the preceding chapters to address classroom incivilities of students more directly. We also present an overview of some of the proposed policies and practices that administrators and institutional committees might consider to supplement policies and procedures that exist on many campuses to deal with research and scholarly misconduct, suggesting expanding the focus of such policies to address faculty misconduct in the collegiate teaching role directly.

Student-Oriented Practices. Student handbooks, codes of conduct, or similar documents rarely provide an expansive treatment of institutional standards regarding civility and incivility in the instructional context and in relation to fellow learners and students' teachers. These documents generally include discussion of cheating and plagiarism, but many fail to go much beyond this treatment of academic misconduct. Student handbooks should expressly mention even relatively minor prohibited acts that may be discourteous or disruptive to other learners and to the instructors—such as taking cell phone calls during class session, reading newspapers or sleeping in an obtrusive manner, arriving late to class or leaving early, emitting audible sounds of disapproval for comments made by other students or by the instructor, making comments demeaning to another student or to a category of individuals, audibly conversing with others in a way that disrupts appropriate student classroom discussion and the remarks of the instructor, and engaging in a virtually infinite variety of other incivilities. Of course, all such possible acts defy cataloguing, so a statement in these student documents should expressly note that those addressed are illustrative and not exhaustive of prohibited student classroom incivilities.

As noted in Chapter Four, "Incidence and Student Response to Faculty Teaching Norm Violations," student handbooks might advisedly include a statement of core normative standards for faculty in the instructional role and the procedures for students to report teaching misbehavior. The student handbook should make it easy for students to determine where and how to make such reports, while assuring student confidentiality.

A somewhat indirect means of identifying normative standards for faculty is by including in student handbooks statements of students' rights regarding their classroom experience and relationship with their instructional faculty members. Chapter Nine, "Promulgating Statements of Student Rights and Responsibilities," lists a number of illustrative items that could properly be stated in this manner. The legitimation of these appropriate expectations by students of their teachers through explication of rights may encourage students to be more active in filing relevant grievances. Students might otherwise be uncertain of what is appropriate and inappropriate pedagogy or may fear intimidation and feel powerless. It should be noted, however, that institutional representatives need to craft these statements and grievance processes in such a way as not to encourage an overly litigious environment, which itself might be detrimental to the educational process.

Faculty Policies. One of the purposes of this volume is to document the often central role that an instructional faculty member plays, both purposely and inadvertently, in creating climates of incivility. Braxton and Bayer (1999) have shown that there are substantial sets of clusters of faculty behaviors in their teaching role that the professoriate—across institutions and across disciplines—generally regard as inappropriate. Indeed, there is general consensus among college and university faculties that there are a number of inappropriate activities by instructional faculty members that merit formal administrative intervention.

Chapter Four, "Incidence and Student Response to Faculty Teaching Norm Violations," among others, chronicles a series of procedures and policies that institutions and faculty senates might consider to strengthen the organization's support for a positive learning environment and to institute a stronger infrastructure to monitor and address faculty misfeasance and malfeasance in the teaching role. They are detailed in some of the preceding chapters and are only summarized below.

- Consistent with advocating the above code of conduct for students, a parallel code of conduct for faculty with respect to instructional behavior might advisedly be developed by individual institutions of higher education and perhaps even by professional associations. Such a code would primarily focus on the professoriate and the teaching role. Some of the primary components of such a code are discussed in Chapter Six, "Toward a Code of Conduct for Undergraduate Teaching."

- Confidential records should be kept on faculty members against whom allegations of teaching misconduct have been brought. The outcome of the investigation and resulting administrative action, if any, should be a part of this record. Maintenance of these records will aid in the detection of

persistent patterns of improprieties, as opposed to current institutional practice, which all too frequently purges these files regardless of judicial findings and actions.

- Institutions should encourage establishment of standing committees
on teaching integrity. Establishment of such a committee formalizes the
institution's and the faculty's commitment to good teaching and to a facili-
tative learning environment. Such formal organizational entities will also
support reporting of improper incidents by individual students and even by
faculty colleagues who may be aware of significant improprieties by a colleague in relation to his or her students.

- Student course-rating instruments, while now broadly used, should be
reviewed by appropriate faculty committees or administrative offices. These
instruments should contain options that readily allow students to provide
information on specific, perceived inappropriate behaviors by the faculty
member in the teaching role, as students are generally in the best position to
observe or experience gross incidents of misfeasance or malfeasance

- Individual institutions and professional academic associations do
little in defining or delineating the appropriate roles and responsibilities
of academic deans and department chairs. Occupants in these positions
generally come from the ranks of the senior instructional faculty, yet they
must define their roles and responsibilities with little guidance beyond
their own personal experiences as rank-and-file faculty members. Among
other responsibilities that might be appropriately codified, these administrators might be expressly and formally charged with overseeing the
integrity of teaching within their unit. It should also be clear that their
role is not solely the protection of the faculty in their unit, but that they
have responsibility to receive and act upon student grievances about
alleged improper behavior of faculty in their instructional roles in an open
and objective manner.

- In respect to the preceding point, departments and colleges should
also formulate policies and procedures, including those roles to be played
by academic deans and department chairpersons, to handle student concerns and complaints pertaining to teaching and classroom incidents.

Next Steps in Researching Incivility in Teaching and Learning Settings

To the present, the discussion of incivilities on the college campus and in
the college classroom has been largely anecdotal and philosophical. To the
degree that research has been conducted on misconduct and incivility in
academe, the focus has been almost exclusively on student improprieties,
and particularly on student cheating and plagiarism. Until the last decade,
with the exception of analyses of research misconduct, virtually no quanti-
tative research has focused on any aspect of faculty improprieties, particularly improprieties in performance of the teaching role.

Moreover, focus on the interplay between faculty incivilities and student incivilities has been virtually neglected. The research work of Boice (1996) is among the first to begin to address this interrelationship. This volume reviews other research work that complements that of Boice and provides new research evidence on teaching and classroom incivilities, particularly in relation to the synergistic dynamics of the interchange between faculty misconduct and that of students and the consequent effects on the teaching and learning environment.

The initial chapters in this volume also provide possible theoretical approaches to guide future research on this topic. To date, virtually all research on incivility at colleges and universities—whether in the campus setting generally or in specific relation to the classroom and the teaching and learning environment—has been atheoretical. Chapter Two, "Sociological Explanations for Faculty and Student Classroom Incivilities," provides a variety of sociological and social-psychological perspectives that may be employed to inform and guide future research on student and faculty misconduct. Chapter Three, "Dynamics of Gender, Ethnicity, and Race in Understanding Classroom Incivility," provides additional theoretical perspective, particularly in respect to the roles that gender and race or ethnicity may play in the dynamics of incivilities between teacher and student.

In addition to advocating more theoretically based research, we propose here some of the next directions for research on incivility in the collegiate teaching and learning environment. Some of these recommendations are based on the limitations to the research reported in this volume; others simply are recommendations for next steps to fill in some of the many gaps in our current research knowledge on the topic.

• Research on such topics as the frequency of faculty teaching norm violations, student responses to faculty teaching norm violations, and the effects of teaching norm violations on the welfare of students should be conducted in non-religiously affiliated comprehensive colleges and universities, liberal arts colleges, and research universities. Such settings might yield a different pattern of findings than that described in this volume.

• Research on the influence of student classroom incivilities on student growth and development should also be extended to non-religiously affiliated comprehensive colleges and universities, liberal arts colleges, and research universities. A different pattern of findings than presented in this volume might result from research in such institutional settings.

• Research on whether undergraduate college students proscribe such patterns of classroom incivilities as disrespectful disruptions and insolent inattention requires attention in types of colleges and universities other than in a highly selective private research university. Further study could also illuminate the types of actions undergraduate students take to deter or sanction such student classroom incivilities.

- In Chapter Six, "Toward A Code of Conduct for Undergraduate Teaching," Braxton and Bayer offer a set of ten tenets that such codes should include. Research could discern whether colleges and universities promulgate such codes of conduct and whether teaching-oriented institutions such as liberal arts colleges and community colleges are more likely to have such codes than research-oriented universities.

- Boice (1996) contends that student classroom incivilities occur because faculty behave inappropriately in class. Bray and Del Favero, in Chapter Two of this volume, also assert that the sociological theories they review posit such a relationship. However, such a linkage remains an open empirical question. Research is needed that seeks to determine the extent to which faculty teaching improprieties foster student classroom incivilities such as insolent inattention and disrespectful disruptions. Research should also address the extent to which student classroom incivilities prompt corresponding faculty teaching transgressions. Classroom observations offer a promising methodological approach to such research.

Conclusions

From the configuration of findings presented in this volume we offer two conclusions. We note that these conclusions are tempered by the limitations of the research described in this volume.

1. Faculty classroom teaching improprieties occur infrequently. Nevertheless, the rate of occurrence for some forms of improprieties—condescending negativism, inattentive planning, and particularistic grading—approximate the rate of research misconduct. Teaching improprieties require social control because of the harm to the academic and intellectual development of students that results from such wrongdoing. Fortunately, undergraduate students assume some measure of responsibility for grievous incidents of faculty teaching-norm violations by either reporting the incident to a dean or department chairperson or by directly talking with the offending faculty member.

2. Like faculty classroom improprieties, student classroom incivilities also negatively affect the academic and intellectual development of students who witness such behaviors. Experience with such behaviors also erodes student commitment to their college or university. However, the possibility that students themselves will exert social control of student classroom incivilities appears uncertain. Undergraduate students tend to disdain such student classroom behaviors as sleeping during class or coming to class intoxicated (insolent inattention), but view less harshly such classroom incivilities as leaving class early, interrupting other students or the professor, or reading the newspaper (disrespectful disruptions). Thus, undergraduate students seem inclined to exercise some social control for insolent inattention, but not for disrespectful disruptions.

Final Thoughts

 Undergraduate students are the primary and most immediate clients of the teaching and learning process of undergraduate education (Braxton and Bayer, 1999). Thus, the protection of the welfare of undergraduate students constitutes an abiding concern of colleges and universities. Faculty adherence to norms of undergraduate teaching safeguards the welfare of students as clients. Thus, individual colleges and universities ought to deter and detect faculty classroom improprieties through implementation of the policies and practices recommended in this concluding chapter and in the other chapters of this volume.

Students who engage in classroom incivilities are acting neither in their own best interest nor in the best interest of their classmates. Likewise, students who tolerate incivilities in the classroom by their peers are also not acting in their own best interest. Students must come to view classroom incivilities as detrimental to their own learning. College and university administrators and faculty should encourage students to act in their own best interest by supporting the promulgation of statements regarding student rights and responsibilities.

College and university administrators, faculty members, and students must shoulder responsibility for the prevention of faculty and student classroom improprieties. Student learning depends on it.

References

Boice, R. "Classroom Incivilities." *Research in Higher Education,* 1996, *37,* 453–485.
Braxton, J. M., and Bayer, A. E. *Faculty Misconduct in Collegiate Teaching.* Baltimore: Johns Hopkins University Press, 1999.

ALAN E. BAYER is professor of sociology, adjunct professor of science studies, and director of the Center for Survey Research at Virginia Polytechnic Institute and State University.

JOHN M. BRAXTON is professor of education in the Higher Education Leadership and Policy Program, Peabody College, Vanderbilt University.

Appendix: Description of Research Methods and Analyses

This Appendix describes the methodology and statistical procedures used to obtain the findings presented in the following chapters of this volume: Chapter Four, "Incidence and Student Response to Faculty Teaching Norm Violations" by Braxton and Mann; Chapter Five, "The Influence of Teaching Norm Violations on the Welfare of Students as Clients of College Teaching," by Braxton, Bayer, and Noseworthy; and Chapter Eight, "Effects of Student Classroom Incivilities on Students," by Hirschy and Braxton. This Appendix also contains the tables referenced in these three chapters as well as in Chapter Seven.

The research described in this Appendix was supported by the Small Faculty Grant Program of Peabody College, Vanderbilt University. The authors of the chapters reporting findings from this research express their appreciation for financial support of this research.

Methodology

Sample and Data Collection. Undergraduate college students in comprehensive colleges and universities-II (CUC-II), baccalaureate colleges (liberal arts colleges)-I (BA-I), and baccalaureate colleges (liberal arts colleges)-II (BA-II) serve as the population of inference for the research reported in these three chapters. These three types of institutions represent categories of the *Classification of Institutions* (1999) produced by Carnegie Foundation for the Advancement of Teaching. The cooperation of five CUC-II, four BA-I, and five BA-II institutions affiliated with a Protestant religious domination was obtained to develop this sample of undergraduate college students. Each of these fourteen institutions randomly selected three hundred students for a total of forty-two hundred students.

NEW DIRECTIONS FOR TEACHING AND LEARNING, no. 99, Fall 2004   © Wiley Periodicals, Inc.

A *National Assessment of College Student Classroom Experience Survey* (the *Survey*) was mailed to each of these students. The survey instrument includes ninety teaching-related behaviors that relate to those inviolable and admonitory normative orientations that students can observe. It also includes items pertaining to student classroom experiences with incivilities by other students, student perceptions of their academic and intellectual development and subsequent commitment to their college or university, as well as items that operationalize pertinent control variables. In addition, an open-ended question appears at the end of the instrument asking respondents to describe the action they took for the most grievous form of faculty classroom misconduct they observed.

Of the 4,200 students mailed the *Survey,* 831 individuals responded with useable survey instruments, for a response rate of 19.8 percent. In spite of a relatively low response rate, the sample obtained is generally representative of the population. Mailing wave analyses indicate no bias on all six of the measures of faculty teaching norm violations. However, bias in the sample toward upperclasspersons (juniors and seniors), full-time students, and female students is detected. Using mailing wave analyses to detect sample bias assumes that later respondents to surveys resemble non-respondents (Goode and Hatt, 1952).

Research Design. The variables used in one or more of the three chapters reporting results include faculty violations of six inviolable and three admonitory norms of undergraduate college teaching, student classroom incivilities, the students' subsequent commitment to their college or university, student perceptions of their academic and intellectual development, and such other variables as gender, class standing, cumulative grade-point average, informal faculty and student interactions, and academic major (in high- and low-consensus disciplines).

Student perceptions of violations of six inviolable and three admonitory norms were measured by asking respondents to indicate how frequently they had observed such behavior in their classes during the current academic year. A four-point response scale was provided: 0 = never, 1 = rarely, 2 = occasionally, and 3 = frequently. Composite indices were computed to measure faculty violations of each of the six inviolable norms and three admonitory norms. These nine indices were developed by summing the responses of students to each behavior of a given normative pattern. The specific behaviors that constitute faculty violations of these nine undergraduate college teaching normative orientations are shown in Table A.1.

Two forms of student classroom incivilities measured are *disrespectful disruptions* and *insolent inattention*. These two measures were empirically delineated through exploratory factor analyses. The factor loadings, alpha reliabilities, and specific types of students' experiences with other students in class that make up these two forms of incivilities are displayed in Table A.2.

Student assessments of their own academic and intellectual development provide an index of the extent to which the interests and welfare of

Table A.1. Faculty Teaching Behaviors Making Up the Measures of Faculty Norm Violations

Measure	Faculty Teaching Behaviors Defining the Measure
Condescending negativism (inviolable)	The following five faculty teaching behaviors observable by students define this norm violation measure: (1) an instructor makes condescending remarks to a student in class, (2) the instructor expresses impatience with a slow learner in class, (3) a faculty member criticizes the academic performance of a student in front of other students, (4) a faculty member treats an advisee in a condescending manner, and (5) instructor does not clearly describe instructions and requirements for course assignments to students.
Inattentive planning (inviolable)	The following two faculty teaching behaviors observable by students define this norm violation measure: (1) the instructor routinely fails to order required texts and other reading materials in time to be available for the first class session, and (2) the instructor routinely fails to prepare a course outline or syllabus for a course.
Moral turpitude (inviolable)	The following three faculty teaching behaviors observable by students define this norm violation measure: (1) a faculty member has a sexual relationship with a student enrolled in the course, (2) a faculty member makes suggestive sexual comments to a student enrolled in the course, and (3) while able to conduct class, the instructor frequently attends class while obviously intoxicated.
Particularistic grading (inviolable)	The following six faculty teaching behaviors observable by students define this norm violation measure: (1) faculty member takes social, personal, or other nonacademic characteristics of students into account in awarding student grades; (2) the instructor allows personal friendship with a student to intrude on the objective grading of his or her work; (3) stated policies about late and incomplete work are not universally applied to all students; (4) students are not permitted to express viewpoints different from those of the instructor; (5) office hours scheduled for student appointments are frequently not kept; and (6) a faculty member neglects to send a letter of recommendation that he or she had agreed to write.
Personal disregard (inviolable)	The following five faculty teaching behaviors observable by students define this norm violation measure: (1) the instructor practices poor personal hygiene and regularly has offensive body odor, (2) the instructor frequently uses profanity in class, (3) class is usually dismissed early, (4) the instructor is routinely late for class meetings, and (5) an instructor lowers course standards in order to be popular with students.
Uncommunicated course details (inviolable)	The following three faculty teaching behaviors observable by students define this norm violation measure: (1) the instructor changes classroom location to another building without informing students in advance, (2) the instructor changes class meeting times without consulting students, and (3) students are not informed of the instructor's policy on missed or make-up examinations.

Table A.1. (Continued) Faculty Teaching Behaviors Making Up the Measures of Faculty Norm Violations

Measure	Faculty Teaching Behaviors Defining the Measure
Inadequate communication (admonitory)	The following eleven faculty teaching behaviors observable by students define this norm violation measure: (1) the instructor does not introduce herself or himself to the class (on the first day), (2) the instructor does not request necessary audiovisual materials in time to be available for class, (3) the first reading assignment is not communicated to the class, (4) assigned books and articles are not put on library reserve by the instructor on a timely basis for student use, (5) the instructor does not ask students if they have any questions regarding the course, (6) office hours are not communicated to students, (7) students are not informed of extra credit opportunities available in the course during the term, (8) the instructor does not return graded tests and papers promptly to students, (9) the instructor does not follow the course outline or syllabus for most of the course, (10) the instructor routinely allows one or a few students to dominate class discussion, and (11) the instructor does not explain the basis for essay questions or papers to students.
Inadequate course design (admonitory)	The following faculty teaching behavior observable by students defines this norm violation measure: required course materials are not kept within reasonable cost limits as perceived by students.
Insufficient syllabus (admonitory)	The following four faculty teaching behaviors observable by students define this norm violation measure: (1) a course outline or syllabus does not contain dates for assignments or examinations, (2) a course outline or syllabus is not prepared and passed out to students, (3) the instructor does not have students evaluate the course at the end of the term, and (4) the instructor does not specify objectives for the course.

Notes: The nine narrative arrays in this table are calculated as composite variables composed of the behaviors listed under each normative pattern. These calculations involve the sum of responses to each behavior divided by the number of behaviors.

Respondents indicate how often each behavior has been personally known to him or her in classes during the current academic year. A four-point response scale is used: 0 = never, 1 = rarely, 2 = occasionally, and 3 = frequently.

students are served. This variable is a composite of five survey items included on the *Survey*. Table A.3 exhibits these five items.

The students' level of subsequent commitment to their college or university was a variable of interest to Hirschy and Braxton in Chapter Eight, "Effects of Student Classroom Incivilities on Students." Table A.3. shows the survey items used to measure this variable.

The findings reported in Chapter Five, "The Influence of Teaching Norm Violations on the Welfare of Students as Clients of College Teaching," and Chapter Eight, "Effects of Student Classroom Incivilities on Students," are above and beyond the influence of the following five control variables:

Table A.2. Factor Loadings and Reliabilities for Classroom Incivilities

National Assessment of College Student Classroom Experience Items

Disrespectful Disruptions (DRESPECT)	Alpha Reliability:	0.81
A student repeatedly interrupts others during the class session		0.76
A student talks loudly to another student while someone else is speaking in class		0.75
A student regularly leaves the class before the class has been excused		0.69
A student makes sarcastic comments or disapproving groans to the teacher		0.69
A student asks confrontational and argumentative question in class		0.60
A student routinely arrives late for class		0.58
A student routinely reads a newspaper or magazine during class		0.49
A student receives cell phone calls or pages during class		0.44
Insolent Inattention (INSOLENT)	Alpha Reliability:	0.70
A student comes to class obviously intoxicated		0.89
A student comes to class obviously high on drugs		0.85
A student sleeps during class		0.55

gender, class standing, cumulative grade-point average, informal faculty and student interactions, and academic major (dichotomized into high- or low-consensus discipline or field). These five variables represent possible rival hypotheses to the influence of norm violations on student academic and intellectual development. Previous research that has focused on student academic and intellectual development has addressed the role of gender, academic discipline, and informal faculty-student interactions as possible sources of influence (Pike, 1989; Terenzini, Springer, Pascarella, and Nora, 1995; Terenzini, Pascarella, and Lorang, 1982; Volkwein and Carbone, 1994; Strauss and Volkwein, 2002). As a consequence, controls for these variables were introduced. Class standing was also controlled, as it is reasonable to expect that juniors and seniors will perceive greater levels of academic and intellectual development than will first-year students and sophomores. Students with higher cumulative grade-point averages are also more likely to perceive greater levels of academic and intellectual development. Table A.3 provides a further description of the construction of these measures.

Statistical Design

Hierarchical linear regression was the statistical procedure used to test the hypothesis advanced in Chapter Five, "The Influence of Teaching Norm Violations on the Welfare of Students as Clients of College Teaching." This statistical procedure was also used to address the research questions posed in Chapter Eight, "Effects of Student Classroom Incivilities on Students."

Table A.3. National Assessment of College Student Classroom Experience Survey Variables

Variables	Definitions
Independent Variables	
Student gender (GENDER)	Male = 1; female = 2
Student class standing (CLASS)	Student's current class level (first year = 1, sophomore = 2, junior = 3, senior = 4)
Student grade point average (GPA)	Current cumulative grade point average on a 4.0 scale (3.5–4.0 = 1; 3.0–3.49 = 2; 2.5–2.99 = 3; 2.0–2.49 = 4; under 2.0 = 5)
Faculty-student interactions (IWF)	Composite variable using five items which include satisfaction with opportunities to interact informally with faculty, development of a close relationship with a faculty member, non-classroom faculty interactions have had positive influence on intellectual growth and interest in ideas; in personal growth, values, and attitudes, and in career goals and aspirations (strongly agree = 1, agree = 2, disagree = 3, strongly disagree = 4)
Student academic major (PDM)	Low-consensus fields (e.g., arts and humanities, business, education, social sciences) = 1; high-consensus fields (e.g., biological sciences, engineering, mathematical/computational sciences, physical sciences) = 2
Institutional type (TYPE)	Carnegie Classification of institution. Baccalaureate colleges (liberal arts colleges)-II (BA-II) = 1; baccalaureate colleges (liberal arts colleges)-I (BA-I) = 2; comprehensive colleges and universities-II (CUC-II) = 3
Disrespectful disruptions (DRESPECT)	Composite variable using ten items (see Table A.2)
Insolent inattention (INSOLENT)	Composite variable using three items (see (Table A.3)
Dependent Variables	
Academic and intellectual development (ACAD)	Composite variable using five items which include satisfaction with academic experience, satisfaction with intellectual development, increase in intellectual matters, intellectual growth and interest in ideas, and academic performance met self expectations (strongly agree = 1, agree = 2, disagree = 3, strongly disagree = 4)
Subsequent commitment to the institution (IC2)	Level of confidence that student made the right decision in choosing the institution (strongly agree = 1, agree = 2, disagree = 3, strongly disagree = 4)

Table A.4. Influence of Violations of Inviolable Teaching Norms on Student Academic and Intellectual Development (ACAD)

Variables	ACAD (CN)[1]	ACAD (IP)	ACAD (PD)	ACAD (PG)	ACAD (UCD)
Gender	−.16	−.25	−.12	−.19	−.22
	(.30)	(−.04)	(−.02)	(−.03)	(−.03)
Class standing	−.26**	−.22**	−.20**	−.26**	−.20**
	(−.09)	(−.08)	(−.07)	(−.09)	(.19)
Academic major	.23	.19	.21	.25	.25
	(.03)	(.03)	(.03)	(.03)	(.03)
Interaction with faculty	.36**	.39**	.38**	.36**	.38**
	(.39)	(.41)	(.40)	(.39)	(.41)
GPA	.59**	.62**	.67**	.62**	.61**
	(.18)	(.19)	(.21)	(.19)	(.19)
Violation of focal norm	1.73**	.68**	1.58**	1.67**	1.33**
	(.30)	(.16)	(.23)	(.28)	(.22)
R^2	.37**	.31**	.34**	.36**	.33**

Notes: Unstandardized regression coefficients are given.

[1]Focal norms: CN = Condescending negativism, IP = Inattentive planning, PD = Personal disregard, PG = Particularistic grading, UCD = Uncommunicated course details.

**Statistically significant at .01 level.

Both chapters used the .05 level of statistical significance to identify statistically reliable findings.

More specifically, the authors of Chapter Five estimated eight regression equations, one for each of the eight measures of faculty norm violations.[1] Specifically, they regressed academic and intellectual development on the five control variables and then on one of the eight norm violations.[2] Table A.4 displays the results of the regression of academic and intellectual development on faculty violations of the five inviolable normative orientations. Table A.5 presents the results of the regression of academic and intellectual development on faculty violations of the three admonitory normative patterns.

In Chapter Eight, the authors estimated four regression equations to determine the influence of the two forms of student classroom incivilities—insolent inattention and disrespectful disruptions—on academic and intellectual development and on subsequent institutional commitment. More specifically, they regressed academic and intellectual development and subsequent institutional commitment on the five control variables and then on the frequency of student experience with insolent inattention and disrespectful disruptions. Table A.6 exhibits the results of these four regression analyses.

Table A.5. Influence of Admonitory Teaching Norm Violations on Student Intellectual and Academic Development (ACAD)

Variables	ACAD (IC)[1]	ACAD (ICD)	ACAD (IS)
Gender	−.24	−.24	−.23
	(−.04)	(−.04)	(−.04)
Class standing	−.26**	−.24**	−.23**
	(.10)	(−.09)	(−.09)
Academic major	.24	.21	.23
	(.03)	(.03)	(.03)
Interaction with faculty	.36**	.40**	.38**
	(.38)	(.42)	(.41)
GPA	.61**	.62**	.62**
	(.19)	(.19)	(.19)
Violation of focal norm	1.83**	.33**	1.13**
	(.29)	(.12)	(.20)
R^2	.36**	.30**	.33**

Notes: Unstandardized regression coefficients; standardized regression coefficients shown in parentheses.

[1]Focal norms: IC = inadequate communication, ICD = inadequate course design, IS = insufficient syllabus.

**Statistically significant at .01 level.

Limitations

Three primary limitations temper the strength of the conclusions advanced in Chapters Four, Five, and Eight. The first limitation pertains to the low response rate to the mailed *Survey*. Although a response rate of only 19.8 percent was obtained, this sample is unbiased with respect to all of the major variables, with the exception of gender and class standing. Thus, the obtained sample appears to be representative of the population of inference.

The second limitation relates to the measurement of academic and intellectual development. This variable is measured cross-sectionally. Stronger inferences about the influence of faculty norm violations and student classroom incivilities on student perceptions of their academic and intellectual development might result from the use of a longitudinal panel of students.

The third limitation concerns the population of inference used in this study, as described earlier. A different pattern of findings might result if undergraduate college students enrolled in other categories of institutions of the Carnegie Foundation's *Classification of Institutions* (1999) were used as the population of inference. Likewise, a different pattern might occur if the population of inference comprised undergraduate students enrolled in non-religiously affiliated colleges and universities of all the categories of the *Classification of Institutions*.

Table A.6. Mean, Standard Deviation, and Reliability Alpha for Variables and Results of Regression Analyses, with ACAD and IC2 as Dependent Variables

Variables	Mean	SD	Alpha	INSOLENT ACAD (n = 776)		INSOLENT IC2 (n = 781)		DRESPECT ACAD (n = 776)		DRESPECT IC2 (n = 781)	
				B	Beta	B	Beta	B	Beta	B	Beta
Independent Variables:											
GENDER	1.70			-0.29	-0.05	-0.09	-0.47	-0.18	-0.29	-0.06	-0.03
CLASS	1.59			-0.36	-0.05	-0.04	-0.02	-0.25	-0.04	-0.01	-0.003
GPA	1.91	0.91		0.61	0.19***	-0.002	-0.002	0.59	-0.18***	-0.01	-0.01
IWF	9.48	3.16	0.85	0.41	0.43***	0.10	0.33***	0.40	0.42***	0.01	0.32
PDM	2.50			0.08	0.08**	0.007	0.02	0.07	0.07*	0.003	0.01***
DRESPECT	1.14	0.54	0.81	1.16	0.21***	0.32	0.19***	0.60	0.11**	0.16	0.09**
INSOLENT	0.53	0.69	0.70					0.99	0.21***	0.28	0.19***
TYPE	2.00	0.81									
(Constant)					3.89		0.74		3.00		0.63
Dependent Variables:											
ACAD	8.88	2.98	0.84								
IC2	1.83	0.93									
Regressions											
Multiple R					0.59		0.40		0.61		0.43
R²					0.34		0.16		0.37		0.19
Adjusted R²				0.34		0.16		0.37		0.18	
Standard error					2.42		0.85		2.38		0.84
F					66.96***		24.96***		65.67***		26.65***

*p = .05; **p = .01; ***p = .001

In addition to these limitations, a fourth limitation applies to the findings of Chapter Four, "Incidence and Student Response to Faculty Teaching Norm Violations." This limitation applies to student responses to the open-ended question on the *Survey* we used to derive the types of actions taken by students for faculty norm violations. Because this instrument was administered through the mail, it is possible that some students who had experienced norm violations and took some actions failed to describe them. Such students may have chosen not to respond to this question because of either the length of the instrument or the location of this item at the end of the instrument. A different pattern of findings might emerge if this question was asked of students in personal, face-to-face interviews or if it had appeared earlier in the instrument.

Notes

1. Braxton, Bayer, and Noseworthy identified two measures of faculty norm violations as highly skewed (measure of skewness equal to or greater than 2.00): uncommunicated course details and moral turpitude. Because highly skewed variables inordinately affect the estimation of regression coefficients, they reduced the skewness of these two measures through logarithmic transformations. Through these logarithmic transformations, only faculty violations of the normative pattern of uncommunicated course details was reduced to an acceptable level of skewness. Consequently, the authors eliminated faculty violations of the proscriptive normative cluster, described by Braxton and Bayer (1999) as moral turpitude, from consideration and in the subsequent statistical analyses.
2. As indicated in the first note, Braxton, Bayer, and Noseworthy conducted a logarithmic transformation of the variable addressing faculty violations of the normative pattern of uncommunicated course details. However, Table A.5 shows the regression coefficient for this variable on its original metric to facilitate the interpretation of this coefficient. The value of the coefficients varies little between the two scales of measurement.

References

Braxton, J. M., and Bayer, A. E. *Faculty Misconduct in Collegiate Teaching.* Baltimore: Johns Hopkins University Press, 1999.

Carnegie Foundation for the Advancement of Teaching. *A Classification of Institutions of Higher Education.* Princeton: Princeton University Press, 1999.

Goode, W. J., and Hatt, P. K. *Methods of Social Research.* New York: McGraw-Hill, 1952.

Pike, G. R. "Background, College Experiences, and the ACT-Comp Exam: Using Construct Validity to Evaluate Assessment Instruments." *Review of Higher Education,* 1989, *13,* 91–117.

Strauss, L. C., and Volkwein, J. F. "Comparing Student Performance and Growth in 2- and 4-Year Institutions." *Research in Higher Education,* 2002, *43,* 133–161.

Terenzini, P. T., Pascarella, E. T., and Lorang, W. G. "An Assessment of the Academic and Social Influences on Freshman Year Educational Outcomes." *Review of Higher Education,* 1982, *5,* 86–110.

Terenzini, P. T., Springer, L., Pascarella, E. T., and Nora, A. "Influences Affecting the Development of Students' Critical Thinking Skills." *Research in Higher Education,* 1995, *36,* 23–39.

Volkwein, J. F., and Carbone, D. A. "The Impact of Departmental Research and Teaching Climates on Undergraduate Growth and Satisfaction." *Journal of Higher Education,* 1994, *65,* 147–167.

INDEX

Academic and intellectual development: peer effects on, 69; and student misconduct, 69–71; student perceptions of, 70–71; and teaching norm adherence/violations, 44

Academic norms, 60–61; for undergraduate college teachers, 49–54 61

Administration, and teaching misconduct, 53

Akers, R. L., 9, 11, 12, 13, 16, 17

Alexander-Snow, M., 21

Alfie, K., 24

Amada, G., 59, 60, 64, 67, 71

Anderson, M. S., 38, 39

Anomie theory, 13, 15, 18

Appleby, D. C., 59, 67

Aries, E., 23

Astin, A. W., 69

Banks, J., 23

Barraclough, R. A., 29

Bayer, A. E., 3, 5, 6, 9, 10, 18, 35, 36, 39, 41, 42, 43, 45, 47, 48, 49, 50, 51, 60, 61, 62, 64, 67, 77, 79, 80, 89, 91, 95

Benton, T. H., 77

Berk, R., 60

Best, J. R., 59

Bjorklund, S. A., 69

Blau, P., 14

Boice, R., 3, 6, 9, 10, 14, 18, 21, 22, 25, 26, 28, 47, 59, 60, 62, 64, 67–68, 71, 73, 74, 77, 89–90, 94

Boren, M. E., 10

Boyer, E., 67

Braxton, J. M., 3, 5, 6, 9, 10, 18, 35, 36, 39, 41, 42, 43, 47, 48, 49, 50, 51, 60, 61, 62, 64, 65, 67, 70, 72, 79, 80, 89, 91, 95

Bray, N. J., 9

Caboni, T. C., 59, 61, 62, 65

Cahn, S. M., 79

Campbell, S. E., 69

Carbone, D. A., 69, 101

Cheating: causes of, 10; and deterrence theory, 11; efforts to define, 82–83; and peer attachment effects, 15

Chickering, A. W., 61, 67, 72

Classroom behavior(s): contract, 82, 83–84; and normative incongruence, 64; peer group influence on, 60–63; and student characteristics, 61, 63; student norms of, 62–65

Classroom decorum, and student codes of conduct, 85

Classroom environment, faculty impact on, 43, 69, 73

Classroom incivilities: aids to addressing, 78–87; broad categories of, 62; and campus policies, 64; and cultural perceptions, 22, 24–25, 27–28; examples and ranking of, 67–68; and institutional type, 70, 72; and interdependent exchanges of value, 14; multicultural perspective on, 25–28; nature of, 10; negative impacts of, 21–22, 71–72; patterns of, 68; and power dynamics, 29–30; prevalence of, 60; prevention, 73; strategies for recognizing and mitigating, 28–30, 71, 73–74; and student departure, 72; synergistic dynamic of, 77–78; and teacher presentation, 22, 26–27

Classroom norm violations, behaviors viewed as, 10, 62

Colbeck, C. L., 69

Communication stereotypes, 24–25

Conflict theory, 16–17, 18

Counseling, 73

Course and teacher evaluations, 15; as student right, 81

Course planning and design principles, 49–50

Course-rating instruments, teaching norms in, 52–53

Crawford, M., 24

Cultural perceptions: and classroom dynamics, 25–26; defined by stereotypes, 24, 25; and social power, 24–25; and teacher immediacies, 26–27

Culture: defined, 23–24; role of communication in, 23

Dalton, J. C., 77

Decoo, W., 47

Del Favero, M., 9

Deterrence theory, 11–12, 18

Back Issue/Subscription Order Form

Copy or detach and send to:
Jossey-Bass, A Wiley Imprint, 989 Market Street, San Francisco CA 94103-1741

Call or fax toll-free: Phone 888-378-2537 6:30AM – 3PM PST; Fax 888-481-2665

Back Issues: Please send me the following issues at $27 each
(Important: please include ISBN number with your order.)

_____

_____

_____

$ _____   Total for single issues

$ _____   SHIPPING CHARGES: SURFACE   Domestic Canadian
                              First Item $5.00 $6.00
                              Each Add'l Item $3.00 $1.50
             For next-day and second-day delivery rates, call the number listed above.

Subscriptions   Please __ start __ renew my subscription to *New Directions for Teaching and Learning* for the year 2___ at the following rate:

U.S.	__ Individual $80	__ Institutional $170
Canada	__ Individual $80	__ Institutional $210
All Others	__ Individual $104	__ Institutional $244
Online Subscription		__ Institutional $170

**For more information about online subscriptions visit
www.interscience.wiley.com**

$ _____   Total single issues and subscriptions (Add appropriate sales tax for your state for single issue orders. No sales tax for U.S. subscriptions. Canadian residents, add GST for subscriptions and single issues.)

__Payment enclosed (U.S. check or money order only)
__VISA __ MC __ AmEx #_____ Exp. Date _____

Signature _____ Day Phone _____
__ Bill Me (U.S. institutional orders only. Purchase order required.)

Purchase order # _____
                Federal Tax ID13559302   **GST 89102 8052**

Name _____

Address _____

_____

Phone _____ E-mail _____

For more information about Jossey-Bass, visit our Web site at www.josseybass.com

NEW DIRECTIONS FOR TEACHING AND LEARNING IS NOW AVAILABLE ONLINE AT WILEY INTERSCIENCE

What is Wiley InterScience?

Wiley InterScience is the dynamic online content service from John Wiley & Sons delivering the full text of over 300 leading scientific, technical, medical, and professional journals, plus major reference works, the acclaimed Current Protocols laboratory manuals, and even the full text of select Wiley print books online.

What are some special features of Wiley InterScience?

Wiley Interscience Alerts is a service that delivers table of contents via e-mail for any journal available on Wiley InterScience as soon as a new issue is published online.

EarlyView is Wiley's exclusive service presenting individual articles online as soon as they are ready, even before the release of the compiled print issue. These articles are complete, peer-reviewed, and citable.

CrossRef is the innovative multi-publisher reference linking system enabling readers to move seamlessly from a reference in a journal article to the cited publication, typically located on a different server and published by a different publisher.

How can I access Wiley InterScience?

Visit http://www.interscience.wiley.com.

Guest Users can browse Wiley InterScience for unrestricted access to journal tables of contents and article abstracts, or use the powerful search engine.

Registered Users are provided with a *Personal Home Page* to store and manage customized alerts, searches, and links to favorite journals and articles. Additionally, Registered Users can view free online sample issues and preview selected material from major reference works.

Licensed Customers are entitled to access full-text journal articles in PDF, with select journals also offering full-text HTML.

How do I become an Authorized User?

Authorized Users are individuals authorized by a paying Customer to have access to the journals in Wiley InterScience. For example, a university that subscribes to Wiley journals is considered to be the Customer. Faculty, staff and students authorized by the university to have access to those journals in Wiley InterScience are Authorized Users. Users should contact their library for information on which Wiley journals they have access to in Wiley InterScience.

ASK YOUR INSTITUTION ABOUT WILEY INTERSCIENCE TODAY!

United States Postal Service

Statement of Ownership, Management, and Circulation

1. Publication Title	2. Publication Number	3. Filing Date
New Directions For Teaching And Learning	0 2 7 1 – 0 6 3 3	10/1/04

4. Issue Frequency	5. Number of Issues Published Annually	6. Annual Subscription Price
Quarterly	4	$170.00

7. Complete Mailing Address of Known Office of Publication (Not printer) (Street, city, county, state, and ZIP+4)

Wiley Subscription Services, Inc. at Jossey-Bass, 989 Market Street, San Francisco, CA 94103

Contact Person
Joe Schuman

Telephone
(415) 782-3232

8. Complete Mailing Address of Headquarters or General Business Office of Publisher (Not printer)

Wiley Subscription Services, Inc. 111 River Street, Hoboken, NJ 07030

9. Full Names and Complete Mailing Addresses of Publisher, Editor, and Managing Editor (Do not leave blank)

Publisher (Name and complete mailing address)

Wiley, San Francisco, 989 Market Street, San Francisco, CA 94103-1741

Editor (Name and complete mailing address)

Marilla D. Svinicki, Center for Teaching Effectiveness/Univ. of Austin, Main Bldg. 2200, Austin, Tx 78712-1111

Managing Editor (Name and complete mailing address)

None

10. Owner (Do not leave blank. If the publication is owned by a corporation, give the name and address of the corporation immediately followed by the names and addresses of all stockholders owning or holding 1 percent or more of the total amount of stock. If not owned by a corporation, give the names and addresses of the individual owners. If owned by a partnership or other unincorporated firm, give its name and address as well as those of each individual owner. If the publication is published by a nonprofit organization, give its name and address.)

Full Name	Complete Mailing Address
Wiley Subscription Services, Inc.	111 River Street, Hoboken, NJ 07030
(see attached list)	

11. Known Bondholders, Mortgagees, and Other Security Holders Owning or Holding 1 Percent or More of Total Amount of Bonds, Mortgages, or Other Securities. If none, check box. → ☑ None

Full Name	Complete Mailing Address
None	

12. Tax Status (For completion by nonprofit organizations authorized to mail at nonprofit rates) (Check one)
The purpose, function, and nonprofit status of this organization and the exempt status for federal income tax purposes:
☐ Has Not Changed During Preceding 12 Months
☐ Has Changed During Preceding 12 Months (Publisher must submit explanation of change with this statement)

PS Form 3526, October 1999 (See Instructions on Reverse)

---

13. Publication Title		14. Issue Date for Circulation Data Below
New Directions For Teaching And Learning		Spring 2004

15.	Extent and Nature of Circulation	Average No. Copies Each Issue During Preceding 12 Months	No. Copies of Single Issue Published Nearest to Filing Date
a.	Total Number of Copies (Net press run)	1952	2066
b. Paid and/or Requested Circulation	(1) Paid/Requested Outside-County Mail Subscriptions Stated on Form 3541. (Include advertiser's proof and exchange copies)	932	901
	(2) Paid In-County Subscriptions Stated on Form 3541 (Include advertiser's proof and exchange copies)	0	0
	(3) Sales Through Dealers and Carriers, Street Vendors, Counter Sales, and Other Non-USPS Paid Distribution	0	0
	(4) Other Classes Mailed Through the USPS	0	0
c.	Total Paid and/or Requested Circulation (Sum of 15b. (1), (2),(3),and (4)) ▶	932	901
d. Free Distribution by Mail (Samples, complement ary, and other free)	(1) Outside-County as Stated on Form 3541	0	0
	(2) In-County as Stated on Form 3541	0	0
	(3) Other Classes Mailed Through the USPS	0	0
e.	Free Distribution Outside the Mail (Carriers or other means)	57	85
f.	Total Free Distribution (Sum of 15d. and 15e.) ▶	57	85
g.	Total Distribution (Sum of 15c. and 15f) ▶	989	986
h.	Copies not Distributed	963	1080
i.	Total (Sum of 15g. and h.) ▶	1952	2066
j.	Percent Paid and/or Requested Circulation (15c. divided by 15g. times 100)	94%	91%

16. Publication of Statement of Ownership
☑ Publication required. Will be printed in the Fall 2004 issue of this publication. ☐ Publication not required.

17. Signature and Title of Editor, Publisher, Business Manager, or Owner | Date

Susan E. Lewis, VP & Publisher – Periodicals | *E. Lewis* | 10/01/04

I certify that all information furnished on this form is true and complete. I understand that anyone who furnishes false or misleading information on this form or who omits material or information requested on the form may be subject to criminal sanctions (including fines and imprisonment) and/or civil sanctions (including civil penalties).

Instructions to Publishers

1. Complete and file one copy of this form with your postmaster annually on or before October 1. Keep a copy of the completed form for your records.

2. In cases where the stockholder or security holder is a trustee, include in items 10 and 11 the name of the person or corporation for whom the trustee is acting. Also include the names and addresses of individuals who are stockholders who own or hold 1 percent or more of the total amount of bonds, mortgages, or other securities of the publishing corporation. In item 11, if none, check the box. Use blank sheets if more space is required.

3. Be sure to furnish all circulation information called for in item 15. Free circulation must be shown in items 15d, e, and f.

4. Item 15h., Copies not Distributed, must include (1) newsstand copies originally stated on Form 3541, and returned to the publisher, (2) estimated returns from news agents, and (3), copies for office use, leftovers, spoiled, and all other copies not distributed.

5. If the publication had Periodicals authorization as a general or requester publication, this Statement of Ownership, Management, and Circulation must be published; it must be printed in any issue in October or, if the publication is not published during October, the first issue printed after October.

6. In item 16, indicate the date of the issue in which this Statement of Ownership will be published.

7. Item 17 must be signed.

Failure to file or publish a statement of ownership may lead to suspension of Periodicals authorization.

PS Form 3526, October 1999 (Reverse)